Macmillan Modern Dramatists
Series Editors: *Bruce King and Adele King*

Published titles

Reed Anderson, *Federico García Lorca*
Eugene Benson, *J. M. Synge*
Renate Benson, *German Expressionist Drama*
Normand Berlin, *Eugene O'Neill*
Michael Billington, *Alan Ayckbourn*
John Bull, *New British Political Dramatists*
Denis Calandra, *New German Dramatists*
Neil Carson, *Arthur Miller*
Maurice Charney, *Joe Orton*
Ruby Cohn, *New American Dramatists, 1960–1980*
Bernard F. Dukore, *Harold Pinter*
Bernard F. Dukore, *American Dramatists, 1918–1945*
Arthur Ganz, *George Bernard Shaw*
Frances Gray, *John Arden*
Julian Hilton, *Georg Büchner*
Helene Keyssar, *Feminist Theatre*
Charles R. Lyons, *Samuel Beckett*
Susan Bassnett-McGuire, *Luigi Pirandello*
Leonard C. Pronko, *Eugène Labiche and Georges Feydeau*
Jeannette L. Savona, *Jean Genet*
Theodore Shank, *American Alternative Theatre*
James Simmons, *Sean O'Casey*
David Thomas, *Henrik Ibsen*
Thomas R. Whitaker, *Tom Stoppard*
Nick Worrall, *Nikolai Gogol and Ivan Turgenev*
Katharine Worth, *Oscar Wilde*

Further titles in preparation

MACMILLAN MODERN DRAMATISTS

JOE ORTON

Maurice Charney

Professor of English
Rutgers University

MACMILLAN

First published 1984 by
THE MACMILLAN PRESS LTD
London and Basingstoke
Companies and representatives throughout the world

Typeset by
Wessex Typesetters Ltd
Frome, Somerset

Printed and bound in Great Britain at
The Camelot Press Ltd, Southampton

British Library Cataloguing in Publication Data
Charney, Maurice
Joe Orton.—(Macmillan modern dramatists)
1. Orton, Joe—Criticism and interpretation
I. Title
822'.914   PR6065.R72/

ISBN 0–333–29202–2
ISBN 0–333–29203–0 Pbk

For
Pauli
'An aged interpreter, though young in
days.'

Contents

List of Plates   viii
Editors' Preface   xi
Acknowledgements   xii
1   Introduction: The Life and Theatrical Career of Jo
    Orton   1
2   Sardonic Intellectualising in *Head to Toe*   29
3   Stylistic Experiments: *The Ruffian on the Stair*,
    Funeral Games, Until She Screams   45
4   Authority and Entertainment in *The Good and
    Faithful Servant* and *The Erpingham Camp*   57
5   Occulted Discourse and Threatening Nonsense in
    Entertaining Mr. Sloane   70
6   *Loot* as Quotidian Farce: The Intersection of
    Black Comedy and Daily Life   80
7   What Did the Butler See in *What the Butler Saw?*   97
8   Farce and Panic in *Up Against It*   111
9   Conclusion: The Ortonesque   123
    References   134
    Bibliography   138
    Index   141

List of Plates

1   Orton and Halliwell's flamboyant collage for the Arden edition of *Antony and Cleopatra*, published by Methuen, and for the *Collins Guide to Roses*

2a The ex-priest McCorquodale (Bill Fraser) outfacing the police in the Yorkshire Television production of *Funeral Games*, 1968. Courtesy: Yorkshire Television

2b Caulfield (Ian McShane) the Private Eye, interrogating Tessa (Vivien Merchant) in *Funeral Games*. Courtesy: Yorkshire Television

3   The Bacchic entertainments in *The Erpingham Camp*, with Erpingham officiating in full dress. Kings Head Theatre, London, 1979. © Donald Cooper

4   The marriage ceremony at the end of the film version of *Entertaining Mr Sloane* (1969), directed by Douglas Hickox, in which Ed (Harry Andrews) and his sister Kath (Beryl Reid) discover a beautiful solution to their sexual problems. Peter McEnery as Sloane. Courtesy: Thorn EMI

5   Beryl Reid as Kath inveigling the young Sloane (Malcolm McDowell) in her grandoise plans for the future. Royal Court Theatre, London, 1975. © Donald Cooper

6   Mr McLeavy (Milo O'Shea) appears to instruct the canny Inspector Truscott (Richard Attenborough) in the film version of *Loot*, 1970. An Arthur Lewis production for British Lion. Courtesy: Thorn EMI

7   Nurse Fay settles on Dennis for her new husband. *Loot*, 1970. Courtesy: Thorn EMI

8   Mrs Prentice (Betty Marsden) expostulating with the imperturbable Dr Rance (Valentine Dyall) who has just placed Geraldine (Jane Carr), in a strait-jacket in *What the Bulter Saw*, Royal Court Theatre, London, 1975. © Donald Cooper

Editors' Preface

The *Macmillan Modern Dramatists* is an international series of introductions to major and significant nineteenth- and twentieth-century dramatists, movements and new forms of drama in Europe, Great Britain, America and new nations such as Nigeria and Trinidad. Besides new studies of great and influential dramatists of the past, the series includes volumes on contemporary authors, recent trends in the theatre and on many dramatists, such as writers of farce, who have created theatre 'classics' while being neglected by literary criticism. The volumes in the series devoted to individual dramatists include a biography, a survey of the plays, and detailed analysis of the most significant plays, along with discussion, where relevant, of the political, social, historical and theatrical context. The authors of the volumes, who are involved with theatre as playwrights, directors, actors, teachers and critics, are concerned with the plays as theatre and discuss such matters as performance, character interpretation and staging, along with themes and contexts.

BRUCE KING

ADELE KING

Acknowledgements

The original idea for this book came from my graduate student, Gary Seigel, who first interested me in Orton and whose own attractive study of the sources of Orton's comedy was a doctoral dissertation at Rutgers in 1981. I have also learned a good deal about Orton from the students in my comedy courses; they understand him much more intuitively than I do. My graduate assistant of many years, John Ribar, is also using Orton significantly in his own criticism. I am grateful to my research assistants, Mark Gallaher and Ray Klimek, for all the hard work they have done in libraries and at the xerox machine. Which reminds me not to forget Linda Adams of the English Department at Rutgers and the many favours she has done for me in connection with my Orton project.

Fred Main of the Rutgers Research Council helped me with a trip to England to explore some of the Orton materials. I discovered that he is also an astute critic of Orton's plays. I am grateful to various officials in the Islington Borough Library for speaking to me so frankly

Acknowledgements

and for showing me Orton and Halliwell's library defacements. Looking at these amusing collages in the solemnity
of the library, I found myself vividly recreating the original
scene. Other persons whose insights I have drawn on freely
without further acknowledgement are Jim Koch and Terence Hawkes.

I wish to thank Jeanine Plottel, the publisher of *New
York Literary Forum*, for permission to reproduce, in a
revised form, an essay that originally appeared in that
periodical, and Jill Levenson, the editor of *Modern Drama*,
for permission to use, in a revised form, two essays that
were published there.

The publishers wish to thank Penguin Books Ltd for
permission to quote extracts from John Lahr's *Prick Up
Your Ears*, 1978, Methuen and Co for permission to quote
extracts from the plays of Joe Orton and Margaret Ramsay
for permission to quote extracts from Orton's private
diaries.

1
Introduction:
The Life and Theatrical
Career of Joe Orton

Lives of playwrights tend to resemble their plays in the sense that they are constructed, highly characterised and sharply delineated into scenes. The playwright is the villain-hero of his own life, and in his diaries, notebooks and letters, he speaks in the crisply significant dialogue of his plays. John Lahr's Orton, in his splendid biography, *Prick Up Your Ears* (1978), is a thoroughly histrionic figure, so that it is difficult to separate the drab, asthmatic Leicester boy whose teachers complained 'was semi-literate. He couldn't spell. He couldn't string a sentence together. He couldn't express himself'[1] from the brilliant London playwright of the 1960s, winner of prizes and sought after by television directors, theatrical producers and the Beatles. There is a myth of the writer as celebrity that Orton was eager to promote.

1

Joe Orton began his festive career as John Kingsley Orton on New Year's Day, 1933, at 9 Fayhurst Road, Saffron Lane Estates, Leicester. He was the oldest of four children, two boys and two girls, and he grew up in what was clearly a working-class environment. His plays are highly autobiographical, but the events and characters of real life are farcically distanced and grotesquely stylised. Only in *The Good and Faithful Servant* does Orton deal directly – and almost tragically – with the meaningless and depersonalised life of Buchanan, who, like his father, William Orton, was a colourless, anonymous, friendless and almost unknown victim of the industrial system. In real life, Orton's father was once employed in a shoe factory but he spent most of his career as a low-paid gardener for the city of Leicester, in which service he lost a finger. In *Entertaining Mr. Sloane* the old Dadda, Kemp, is at least querulous and accusatory, and he is not stamped to death by Sloane without giving him a little trouble. Father figures in Orton tend to be either puffed-up tyrants like Erpingham and Dr Rance or mousey little men like his own father – perhaps two sides of the same imaginative coin.

Orton's mother, Elsie, was apparently an irritating, domineering, capricious little woman who made life miserable for all of her children. It is surprising how little affection her death, on 26 December 1966, elicited from any of her family. Elsie worked for a while in the prosperous hosiery industry of Leicester, then later as a charwoman, but what she liked most was to visit her favourite pubs and sing sentimental songs. Her children remember her as a genteel and fussy woman who was also stubborn and not to be crossed. She seems to be remarkably like Kath, the lazy, sensual, very respectable mother-whore in *Entertaining Mr. Sloane*. It is not a flattering portrait, and the intensely homosexual misogyny that runs through the play is a continuing theme in Orton, whose women are either slovenly matriarchs, like Kath, or coldly bossy, phallic temptresses like Nurse Fay in *Loot* or Mrs Vealfoy in *The Good and Faithful Servant*. Again, these sharply opposed characteristics may be two aspects of the same person, and Orton delighted in paradox, contradiction and illogicality. He insisted strenuously that he was writing about real life while blatantly indulging himself in heroic and surrealistic fantasy. He liked the grotesque juxtaposition of real and imaginary events woven together in a seamless fabric, and he made no sharp distinction between real life and the life of the imagination.

All the details of Orton's career are lucidly set forth in Lahr's biography, so that it is my purpose merely to sketch the figure in the carpet and to show a relation between the playwright's life and art. Orton was eager to project various romantic images of himself in his works. He was, most vividly, the young hoodlum and drifter Sloane, who is a wistful, violent, opportunistic, but in some ways very innocent orphan who loves the good things in life. With luxuriant fantasy, Orton compensates for his own deprived background. Sloane's putative parents were 'extremely wealthy people',[2] who died in a suicide pact when he was eight, but who were so overwhelmingly middle class as to verge on parody: 'From what I remember they was respected. You know, H.P. [hire-purchase or instalment] debts. Bridge. A little light gardening. The usual activities of a cultured community' (p. 68). This is the philistine culture of Matthew Arnold. Like Jay Gatsby, Sloane seems to be his own progenitor, without family, roots or any commitments. He appears from nowhere to rent a room and is soon manipulating both Kath and her homosexual brother Ed. Sloane is, in Tennessee Williams' phrase, 'a sweet bird of youth', a fine, self-confident talker able to

3

tease and to cajole with his muscular good looks and working-class charm. If he is also a murderer, he is a very casual one, not from intent but from a psychopathic love of ease and hatred of contradiction.

Impelled by misguided snobbery, Orton's mother sent him to private school, Clark's College, from 1945 to 1947. This was actually a commercial college, in which the reluctant and dull John Orton was being prepared for a career as secretary or clerk in Leicester. He was later to dramatise this phase of his life in the character of Ray, a feckless youth in *The Good and Faithful Servant*, who is forcibly processed into the nameless and faceless corporation. While working at various dead-end office jobs in Leicester, Orton fantasised his escape from his humdrum and routinised life through the theatre. On 13 April 1949, he recorded his secret wishes in his diary:

> Last night sitting in the empty theatre watching the electricians flashing lights on and off, the empty stage waiting for rehearsal to begin, I suddenly knew that my ambition is and has always been to act and act. To be connected with the stage in some way, with the magic of the Theatre and everything it means. I know now I shall *always* want to act and I can no more sit in an office all my life than fly. (Lahr, p. 58)

Orton joined various local dramatic groups – the Leicester Dramatic Society, the Bats Players, the Vaughan Players – hoping for the big part that never came. The role of Tyltyl in Maeterlinck's *The Blue Bird* was his major success, but he was generally typecast in insignificant children and ingénu parts. No one at the time was impressed with Orton's histrionic abilities, yet he nurtured grand ambitions for himself.

4

In late April of 1950 he undertook private elocution lessons with 'Madame' Rothery to eradicate a slight lisp and many Leicesterisms in his speech and to perfect the posh accent that would help him with the auditions for the Royal Academy of Dramatic Art. It is characteristic of Orton's early career that everyone who taught him considered him totally mediocre, colourless, unimaginative and entirely lacking in talent. Orton was right to believe that Madame Rothery 'didn't think much of me, just a yob, I could tell that', because Lahr's interview with her corroborates Orton's fears:

> He was just an ordinary, unsophisticated boy. I was quite staggered he wanted to go on the stage. His people were ordinary working-class people. There was no culture, no education. I felt sorry for him. Here's a boy that wants to do something. He's not got much talent, but I was out to help him.   (Lahr, p. 70)

'Culture' is a code word for class distinctions, yet Orton managed to weather his teacher's patronising contempt and to be accepted at the Royal Academy of Dramatic Art.

He left Leicester for RADA in May 1951, and going to London was the turning-point of his career. He was never a brilliant or memorable student. As an actor he tended to play sentimental comic roles, although he longed to play Puck in *Midsummer Night's Dream* and Ariel in *The Tempest* – he had already played Peter Pan with some success. His range was very limited, and Lucio in *Measure for Measure* for the Vaughan Players in Leicester (July 1951) was his most demanding role. When he completed his training at RADA, Orton worked for a brief period in the spring and summer of 1953 as Assistant Stage Manager of the Ipswich Repertory Company. It became clear that he had no particular calling as stage manager, actor or director, and the first phase of his career in the theatre ended when he went back to live with Kenneth Halliwell, a fellow student at RADA. On Kenneth's modest income, they were both determined to devote their full time to writing novels.

It is easy to malign the depressed, owlish, pretentiously literary and saturnine Halliwell, seven years older than Orton and almost completely bald. Lahr in his biography consistently downplays Orton's room-mate and lover, who must have had a much larger role in Orton's creative development than Lahr allows him. Before Joe became a celebrity, the sophisticated and well-educated Halliwell, a student of the classics, served as mentor and big brother to him and encouraged him to read voraciously and to trust himself as a writer. What began as a collaboration in which Halliwell was dominant, gradually changed into one in which Orton wrote novels in his own name. Despite the evidence of the title-pages, it is still difficult to untangle Orton's share from Halliwell's, especially because Kenneth's perverse and bookish spirit broods over the novels. The titles are romantically prurient: *Priapus in the Shrubbery*, *The Silver Bucket*, *The Mechanical Womb*, *The Last Days of Sodom*, *Between Us Girls* and *The Boy Hairdresser*. It is all meant to be very clever, very superior, and very culturally allusive, with an echo of the esoteric cuteness of Ronald Firbank.[3]

Orton first moved into Halliwell's West Hampstead flat on 16 June 1951, when they were students at RADA, then later moved to the Islington flat that was purchased mostly with Kenneth's small inheritance from his father, who had committed suicide, and his and Joe's savings from their jobs at Cadbury's. In *The Ruffian on the Stair*, written just before *Sloane*, Orton reconstructs his liaison with Kenneth

Halliwell as an intense, incestuous relation between two brothers. Wilson, the younger brother, cannot live now that his older and heavily tattooed brother Frank has been murdered, and he actively seeks his own death at the hands of Mike, the small-time gangster who killed Frank. Orton's account of Wilson's life with his brother is highly autobiographical:

> We lived in Shepherd's Bush. We had a little room. And our life was made quite comfortable by the N.A.B. [National Assistance Board or Welfare] for almost a year. We had a lot of friends. All creeds and colours. But no circumstances at all. We were happy, though. We were young. I was seventeen. He was twenty-three. You can't do better for yourself than that, can you? (*He shrugs.*) We were bosom friends. I've never told anyone that before. I hope I haven't shocked you. (p. 49)

Now that his lover is dead, Wilson is 'a bit lost without him' (p. 59) and 'going round the twist with heartbreak' (p. 50). The mixture of sentiment and farcical bravado is typically Ortonesque. Wilson is a 'Gents hairdresser' who has 'clipped some notable heads' in his time, including an amateur street musician: 'We gave him satisfaction, I believe' (p. 34). The most banal tag-lines cannot conceal Wilson's inability to live without his brother, so that our feelings are at once alienated and exacerbated. All of this grotesque interplay of suicide and murder is prophetic of Orton's own death at the hands of his room-mate, Halliwell, who bashed in his skull with a hammer then killed himself with an overdose of Nembutals.

The events of Orton's life are as bizarre as anything in his plays. From 1959 to 1962, besides being failed actors and novelists, Orton (with Halliwell) stole books from the

7

Islington public libraries, altering the dust jackets and rewriting the blurbs on the inside flap – all to make them both absurd and obscene. They also removed 1653 plates from art books, most of which eventually wound up in the enormous floor-to-ceiling collage in Orton and Halliwell's bed-sitter apartment at 25 Noel Road, Islington, although some were used to embellish the drab covers of the library books. Joe did almost all of the writing, and it would seem that Kenneth took a large hand in the art work. They went at their creations with great skill and devotion, and the Orton/Halliwell collages for the Arden Shakespeare deserve to be reprinted by Methuen in place of their very sombre originals. In burlesque Sherlock Holmes fashion, the culprits were tracked down by Sidney Porrett, the Islington Borough Council's legal clerk; they were charged and tried and both sent to prison for six months.

What gave most offence to the court was a tiny monkey or gibbon unobtrusively pasted in the centre of the beautiful yellow rose on the cover of *Collins Guide to Roses*. This shook the very foundations of English domestic life. As Orton told Giles Gordon, 'What I had done was held up as the depth of iniquity for which I should probably have been birched'.[4] For Orton, sneaking the altered books back into the library and watching the horrified expressions on the faces of the old ladies who whiled away their time there was an experiment in street – or library – theatre. 'I used to stand in corners after I'd smuggled the doctored books back into the library and then watch people read them. It was very funny, very interesting' (p. 98). This was the most serious acting and staging that Orton and Halliwell, both graduates of the Royal Academy of Dramatic Art, had ever done, and it launched Orton on his career as dramatist. For the first time in his life he had a fascinated and captive audience.

Some of the librarians in Islington – slow but sure in their old-fashioned methods of detection, like Inspector Trus-cott in *Loot* – still remember Orton with considerable animus as someone who betrayed his working-class origins, the library books being stepping-stones to one's advance-ment up the rigid class hierarchy. None of them sees anything funny in the episode. Orton and Halliwell went to great artistic and larcenous lengths to take their revenge against the world of books and publishing that spurned them, but six months in prison for what was basically a sophomoric joke seems unduly harsh. As Orton said later when asked about the influence of prison on his writing: 'it affected my attitude towards society. Before, I had been vaguely conscious of something rotten somewhere: prison crystallised this. The old whore society really lifted up her skirts, and the stench was pretty foul.'[5]

None of Halliwell's writing was ever published, although he had a few nibbles from London publishers. He must have continued with his collages, in the style of the book defacements, because in January 1967 he was getting ready for an exhibit at an antique store on King's Road in London. The subjects, as reported by Orton, give some notion of the state of Halliwell's psyche some months before he was brutally to murder his room-mate and take his own life: 'a macabre Venus made of bits of fingers and mouths on a background that looked like a crumbling tube station wall'; 'eggs bursting over a suburban landscape. A negress, cut from a book of African art, lifted up her hands and screamed'; 'a bull made of human hair leaping around in a sandpit and charging [with] three human eyes' (Lahr. p. 241). As Orton became more and more illustrious, Hal-liwell became more perversely pathetic, a mere acolyte of the Great Man. We can understand his paranoid fears that Orton would eventually leave him. At the time of the murder on 9 August 1967, a sour, sarcastic, frustrated and disappointed Halliwell was just on the point of being hospitalised for the nervous breakdown that was over-whelming him.

The only work of fiction to be published from Orton and Halliwell's early years as novelists is *The Vision of Gombold Proval*, probably completed in 1961 (although Orton dates it in 1959[6]). This appeared posthumously in 1971 as *Head to Toe*. Although it is undoubtedly Orton's work, the influence of Halliwell is pervasive in the pseudo-intellectual, wisecracking, polymath and decadent tone, and Halliwell is clearly the model for the owlish Doktor von Pregnant, who undertakes Gombold's education in prison: 'He was tall, with bedraggled hair reaching to his shoulders, deep-set eyes, almost buried beneath thick eyebrows, and a long beard falling to his knees. . . . He looked about 2,000 years old. . . .'[7] Even as a child Kenneth always seemed grave and elderly, an effect much enhanced by his prema-ture baldness (although Doktor von Pregnant is, in revenge, exceptionally hirsute). In many distinctive ways, Halliwell looked and acted the part of Orton's absent father; they are both well qualified for Mel Brooks' and Carl Reiner's 2000-year-old man.

Head to Toe is an extremely detached, end-of-the-world narrative, full of philosophical musings, pedantry, mis-ogyny and sour satire. The anarchic high spirits of Orton's later work are not much evident, yet there is still a sense of fun, especially in the character Offjenkin, the histrionic revolutionary, whose new play 'was the most daring thing ever written. It was about a man and woman who got married' (p. 148). Offjenkin is a campy anarchist with an eye to theatrical effects: 'he organized a march into the city centre wearing a mask and carrying a banner on which nothing was written' (p. 147). Offjenkin's 'attacks' sound more like ideas for dadaist street theatre or happenings than the workings of a political movement: 'Offjenkin and his men filtered back; with much satisfaction telling how the whole village, every man, woman and child, had been stared at. Such incidents, Offjenkin declared, were liable to rock the status quo and tumble any Government from power' (p. 146).

In relation to Orton's development as a dramatist, *Head to Toe* is a mine of material that was to be used later, much transformed, in the plays. It is very directly the source of his film script for the Beatles, *Up Against It* (1967). The novel projects ideas of ambiguous and polymorphous sexuality that were to be taken up in all of Orton's work and especially in *What the Butler Saw* (1967). As the manager of the Consummatum Est brothel puts it to a customer who does not know which sex he prefers: 'We have just the thing for you, sir. Madam Priapus, the female Hercules; two sexes for the price of one' (p. 142). Connie Hogg, the formidable Amazon who is Chief of Police, has made Gombold her wife and speaks to him in prissy, infantalising, transvestite rhetoric: 'You've been a bad girl. A regular little tarty. What did you want to go dressing up in Daddy's clothes for? People will think you are a man' (p. 26). Gombold has 'a pretty, frilly, pinky room'. Although the circumstances are different, the tone is that of Ed upbraiding Sloane in *Entertaining Mr. Sloane*. In the Conference Hall of the ruling gynaecocracy where Gombold goes to assassinate the Prime Minister, he sees 'a column crowned by a lioness holding a cock between its paws. He shuddered at the symbol' (p. 31).

There is a vitality of language that shines through this often effete and precious novel, which is as much about the process of literary composition as about a journey through the body of a dying giant. In prison Gombold has visions of detached images that will form the basis for his writing:

11

Incongruous symbols mixed with holy things: a phallus, a mitre, Hermes the mystagogue who guided souls, a woman lifting her forefinger to her lips; two men locked in a cupboard pointing rods at him. By use of images it might be possible to extract from fantasy a kind of reality. (p. 60)

The images are surprisingly literary and classical (Hermes the thief and the goddess Opportunity who holds a forefinger to her lips), and Orton is beginning to understand the way out of the luxuriant garden of fantasy laid out for him by Ronald Firbank and Lewis Carroll. When the whole landscape comes alive, Gombold sees an 'incongruous monster' and marvels 'at the ingeniousness of its construction evading the obvious' (p. 11). The laughter of the loganberries has a malicious ring to it, and their dialogue is appropriately bitchy:

> 'Oh, I prayed a bit, I admit. You couldn't stop me. But it wasn't prayers that saved me.'
> 'What then?'
> 'It was my thorns.' (p. 12)

Although embedded in a prissy floral animation, the dialogue is dramatic and the speakers are sharply, if briefly, characterised. We could be listening to Nurse Fay in *Loot* or Mrs Vealfoy in *The Good and Faithful Servant*. Orton's *Through the Looking-Glass* world is an allegory for the workings of the imagination.

Orton's career as a playwright began in earnest in 1963 when the BBC Third Programme accepted his one-act play, *The Ruffian on the Stair*. This was originally the highly autobiographical novel, *The Boy Hairdresser*, written with

Halliwell and based on their verse satire of the same name. Orton's third, dramatic version of the novel was radically different from the two that preceded it. Throughout his career, he showed enormous capacity for rewriting and for successfully developing dramatic material from the suggestions and criticisms of others. We know that *Loot* was almost totally rewritten while it was in rehearsal and even while it was being performed outside London. This may have been infuriating to the actors, but Orton's sensitivity to what was wrong on stage was ultimately of great benefit to the play. The process of revision generally cut verbiage – even witty and epigrammatic lines – to strengthen character and stage effect. *The Ruffian on the Stair* that the BBC eventually broadcast, on 31 August 1964, was much transformed from what Orton had originally submitted. The play was again extensively revised for its first theatrical presentation by the English Stage Company at the Royal Court Theatre on 21 August 1966. Orton was embarrassed by the publication of the radio version of *Ruffian* in a BBC collection of *New Radio Drama* (1966). It is much more explicit than the later version and all the comic situations are worked out in fuller and perhaps superfluous detail.

The Ruffian on the Stair was not the first play that Orton wrote. We have the manuscript of *Untitled Play* from 1959, a curiously moralistic and explanatory study of laughter and rage, a topic close to his heart. From 1960 we have his archly salacious skit, *The Patient Dowager*, which he gave Kenneth Tynan – lightly revised and with a new title, *Until She Screams* – for the London version of *Oh! Calcutta!* There is also *The Visit*, from 1961, a short hospital play in which an old man is dying amidst the babble of nurses and his 70-year-old daughter. Both the Royal Court Theatre and the BBC found *The Visit* attractive but rejected it. Orton could always write excellent dialogue, but he needed practice in shaping character and event.

The Ruffian on the Stair shows an enormous debt to Pinter, and, in part, the play is almost a parody of Pinter's early comedies of menace such as *The Birthday Party*, *The Room* and *The Dumb Waiter*. But Orton's *Ruffian* also has a mischievous predilection for farce at the most serious moments that is not like Pinter at all. Thus, in the midst of Wilson's conversation with Mike, in which he is trying to persuade Mike to kill him, Wilson launches into broad-Irish ethnic humour: 'I'd like to see a Liffey man on the throne of St. Peter myself. I'd be proud to hear the Lateran ring with the full-throated blasphemies of our native land' (p. 47). This is the sort of music hall turn that Pinter scrupulously avoided. At the very end of the play Mike fires two shots at close range at Wilson, the first of which crashes into the goldfish bowl. The juxtaposition of the murdered Wilson and the murdered goldfish veers the tragic action into farce. The sympathies of Mike's girlfriend, Joyce, seem to lie entirely with the goldfish: 'They're dead. Poor things. And I reared them so carefully. And while all this was going on they died' (p. 61). Joyce's maternal instincts are grotesquely misplaced, and the play ends with oddly conflicted emotions as Mike announces that he will fetch the police: 'This has been a crime of passion. They'll understand. They have wives and goldfish of their own' (p. 61). Thus what began as melodrama ends as burlesque.

Orton must have been revising *The Ruffian on the Stair* at the same time that he was writing his first full-length play, *Entertaining Mr. Sloane*, between September and December 1963. Both plays owe a large debt to Pinter. *Entertaining Mr. Sloane* and Pinter's *Birthday Party* (1958) have some striking parallels: Orton's heroine, Kath, shares with Pinter's Meg some aspects of the mother/whore role, and Orton's Ed is conceived in the suave style of Pinter's fastidious gangster Goldberg, but Sloane is totally unlike Pinter's Stanley or any Pinter character at all. Orton's protagonist is a combination of ready-made, sloganistic eloquence; a self-indulgent, gigolo's style; and a Teddy boy's playful violence. When he enters the play, he has already committed one casual murder of a benefactor who wanted to photograph him in the nude, and he is well on the way to stamping to death the old, snivelling, querulous Dadda. The farcical viciousness of this play is more in the style of Anthony Burgess' *A Clockwork Orange*, published in 1962, and of Stanley Kubrick's film version in 1972, than anything in Pinter. Both Sloane and Alex are young, sensitive, pleasure-loving psychopaths, who have neither hard feelings nor any recollection of the old ideas of sin, conscience and the reciprocities of the Law of Love. They do understand luxury, pampering, self-indulgence and fast action.

Entertaining Mr. Sloane was first staged at the New Arts Theatre Club on 6 May 1964, and then transferred to a larger theatre in the West End. It was directed by Patrick Dromgoole, whom Orton energetically despised and whom he later satirised in *Up Against It*, the film script for the Beatles, as the bland and conventionally romantic maiden, Miss Drumgoole. *Sloane* is part of Orton's 'Dialectic of Entertainment', in Simon Shepherd's pregnant phrase. The title of the play is sardonic in various senses of the word 'entertaining'. Everyone in the household except the grudging and surly Dadda is busy entertaining the new lodger, Mr Sloane, at the same time that Sloane is entertaining them – relieving their crushing, provincial boredom.

As Orton explained to Alan Schneider, who directed the

Broadway version of the play, Ed and Kath were conceived in tandem as sexual exploiters: Ed's 'stalking of the boy's arse was as funny and as wildly alarming as Kath's stalking of his cock' (Lahr, p. 154). Sloane knows how to ingratiate himself, to make himself desirable and entertaining. All the characters speak in the slick, vapid, moralistic and sentimental clichés of mass entertainment, especially television. They strive to conceal their gross needs beneath a veneer of genteel banter and polite chit-chat, so that even the murder of their old father is processed with the detachment of daytime television. Kath, for example, says: 'What a thing to do. Hit an old man. It's not like you. You're usually so gentle', and 'He can be aggravating I know, but you shouldn't resort to violence, dear' (p. 128). Brother and sister fully agree about Sloane:

> KATH: He's bad, isn't he?
> ED: A very bad boy. (p. 131)

They infantilse their father's cold-blooded murderer for purposes that are not revealed until the end of the play, when the tables are suddenly turned on the wheedling Sloane.

During the run of *Entertaining Mr. Sloane*, Orton wrote a television play, *The Good and Faithful Servant*, completed in June 1964 and broadcast by Rediffusion Television on 6 April 1967. This is his tenderest and most moving play, more a bitter satire on the deadening, dehumanising factory system than a farce. The play is so much a eulogy for Orton's own withered father that it is difficult to integrate it into comedy. The root idea is already present in *Entertaining Mr. Sloane*, when Sloane leaves the orphanage and joins the corporate world:

> They'd found me a likeable permanent situation. Can-

teen facilities. Fortnight's paid holiday. Overtime? Time
and a half after midnight. A staff dance each year. What
more could one wish to devote one's life to?   (p. 124)

This is indeed what the elderly, worn-out Buchanan in *The
Good and Faithful Servant*, who is about to retire, has
devoted his life to. He is pathetic in his total abandonment
and friendlessness, and his gesture of smashing the company's retirement presents, a clock and a toaster that do not
work, is supremely futile. He counts for so little that there is
no way for him to protest against the system. Although only
a commissionaire, or doorman, he has lost an arm in the
service of his corporation, which only confuses the long-lost
girlfriend of his youth, Edith:

EDITH: Your arms! Where has the extra one come from?
BUCHANAN: It's false.
EDITH: Thank God for that. I like to know where I stand
in relation to the number of limbs a man has.

(p. 165)

A snappy, scintillating line, but in this play it only adds to
the gloomy anticipation of Buchanan's death. Without any
speech at all, he *'lies back, stares at the ceiling'*, weeps,
'closes his eyes and dies' (p. 191). He cannot live outside the
company and his retirement is already a symbolic death.

Death in *Loot*, Orton's next full-length play, is a
consistently farcical subject, and the corpse of the late and
not-yet-buried Mrs McLeavy is much manhandled and
displaced. She cannot even manage to retain her glass eye
and false teeth. *Loot*, first written between June and
October 1964, was originally called *Funeral Games*. The
play went through enormous transformations between its
first production at the Arts Theatre in Cambridge on 1
February 1965, and its London version, which opened at

the Jeanetta Cochrane Theatre on 27 September 1966, and later transferred to the Criterion in the West End.

Despite its detective-thriller format and surrealistic style, Orton thought of *Loot* – and of all his plays for that matter – as being intensely realistic, in the sense that they were fundamentally true to human experience, and especially to the psychological realism that he admired in Shakespeare and the classic dramatists. Orton was appalled by the way directors stylised his plays because they could not understand them. Thus Peter Wood's original version at Cambridge failed because he conceived *Loot* as an 'artificial comedy' in Charles Lamb's sense – 'sports of a witty fancy' that make no attempt to imitate 'real life'. Wood later understood his misdirection: 'I tried to do the play with a kind of cod formality as if it were *Way of the World* or something. ... It was a mistake not to have plumped for absolute realism. I was kind of afraid of the play' (Lahr, p. 199). As Orton told his American director, 'Unless *Loot* is directed and acted perfectly seriously, the play will fail' (Lahr, p. 199). This is the same point that Michael Bates, who played Truscott in Marowitz's successful London run, was to make: 'Joe's ideas were often better than the director's. He felt *Loot* should be very real. He would have liked the play more real. He was right. If you've got something extraordinary, you've got to make it believable' (Lahr, p. 217). Although Orton did not actively protest, he thought of Marowitz as pretentious and abstract, and his commercially successful production of *Loot* seemed to Orton painfully wrong.

There is an element of fun and games in *Loot* that seems more self-assured than anything in Orton's previous plays. Inspector Truscott of Scotland Yard is a wonderfully histrionic and self-confident figure. When he proposes to the stuffily respectable McLeavy that they all split the loot, he speaks in the theatrically self-conscious jargon of community standards: 'What has just taken place is perfectly scandalous and had better go no farther than these three walls. It's not expedient for the general public to have its confidence in the police force undermined' (p. 271). But when the unco-operative McLeavy suddenly finds himself arrested, his self-righteousness is scandalised: 'You can't do this. I've always been a law-abiding citizen. The police are for the protection of ordinary people' (p. 274). Truscott has to clue him in to the disagreeable facts of life: 'I don't know where you pick up these slogans, sir. You must read them on hoardings' (p. 274). Similarly, the homicidal Nurse Fay mouths the platitudes of the democratic welfare state: 'I'm innocent till I'm proved guilty. This is a free country. The law is impartial.' Once more, Truscott cuts through the meaningless verbiage: 'Who's been filling your head with that rubbish?' (p. 254). Fay of course agrees, but the stodgy McLeavy protests to the end. *Loot* manages to be funny, licentious and lacerating at the same time. It is a much more relaxed play than anything Orton had written so far.

In the midst of the rewrites for *Loot* in 1965, Orton composed a television play, *The Erpingham Camp*, that is loosely based on Euripides' *The Bacchae*. This was originally a 19-page film treatment – written in 1964 and never used – for Lindsay Anderson, in the Brechtian style of epic narration that also figures in *Up Against It*. Under the influence of Halliwell, Orton loved to cite classical underpinnings for his plays, and *The Bacchae* reappears as a source for *What the Butler Saw*. According to Orton's diary, Halliwell also claimed Sir James Frazer's *Golden Bough* as the subtext for this play (Lahr, p. 21). There is a certain autodidactic puffery and intellectual put-on in Orton's extravagant desire to give his plays a respectable ancestry.

Surely he must have been joking when he told the BBC that
Entertaining Mr. Sloane had Sophocleian roots: 'I got Eddie
the brother and father relationship from *Oedipus at
Colonus* – the old man won't speak to his son at all' (Lahr,
p. 147). *The Erpingham Camp* has plenty of Dionysiac and
Bacchic energy, especially in the revolt of the campers to
the tune of 'La Marseillaise', but its specific relation to *The
Bacchae* is shadowy.

The play was screened by Rediffusion Television on 27
June 1966, and was later staged, in a much revised version,
with *The Ruffian on the Stair* as *Crimes of Passion* (a phrase
from the ending of *Ruffian*), by the English Stage Company
at the Royal Court Theatre, 6–17 June 1967. During the
videotaping, Orton was impressed by the director's
naturalistic style: 'It's been directed and acted absolutely
real. With astonishing results. H. Pinter says it's like *The
Battleship Potemkin*' (Lahr, p. 210). 'Real' is a key word for
Orton, who objected violently to the campy, displaced,
'artificial comedy' interpretations of his plays by actors,
directors and critics. He thought of himself as a writer of
well-made, situation comedies, with well-rounded and not
caricatural characters, who speak in the jejune platitudes
and tired, proverbial formulae of ordinary conversation.
Erpingham was meant to be an entirely credible
businessman and patriotic Briton whose vision of the future
is appropriately sentimental and tawdry:

The shapeliest girls in Britain – picked from thousands of
disappointed applicants. There'll be no shortage of
horses. And heated pools. The accommodation will be
lavish. Slot-machines will be employed for all tasks.
They'll come from far and wide to stay at my entertain-

ment centres. The great ones of this world and, if Fame's trumpet blows long and hard enough, of the next.

(pp. 281–2)

The setting is pure Las Vegas and the rhetoric is Grade B Hollywood extravaganza, with an additional fillip of grandiose hyperbole.

Against Erpingham, the figure of Authority, the bacchanalian Kenny and his pregnant wife Eileen have an irrepressible violence that is equally synthetic. Kenny's revolutionary tirades are in the sloganistic and somewhat archaic mode of patriotic oratory:

> Man does not live by bread alone! It's the small things in life that matter. And I'm prepared to risk a lot for those! . . . We're doing this thing not for ourselves, but for our wives and loved ones – pregnant now and in the times to come, that they may be safe from never knowing where the next meal is coming from. (p.310)

The most resounding line in the play is Kenny's defiance of Erpingham's monarchistic and Tory bluster: 'You'll pay for this, you ignorant fucker!' (p. 307). *The Erpingham Camp* is Orton's most political play, and his attack on the system, although more oblique than *The Good and Faithful Servant*, is nevertheless more powerful. Originally written for the director Lindsay Anderson, *Erpingham* has a satirical energy not unlike the vivacious political allegory of Anderson's recent film, *Britannia Hospital* (1982).

Orton's television play, *Funeral Games*, was written between July and mid-November 1966 and was broadcast on Yorkshire Television on 25 August 1968, a little over a year after his death. Its ostensible theme is Christian

Charity (or the lack thereof), as part of an ITV series on
The Seven Deadly Virtues. Like *Loot*, whose original title
it usurps, *Funeral Games* is a murder mystery and whodunnit, but without any suspense. We know almost from the
start that the defrocked and valetudinarian Catholic priest,
McCorquodale, has murdered his wife Valerie, whose body
lies in the basement 'under a ton of smokeless coal'
purchased 'at the reduced summer rate' (p. 331). Caulfield,
the private eye, is a youthful amateur more like Hal in *Loot*
than Inspector Truscott. His shock – 'You're a murderer?'
– is deflected by the ailing priest: 'These "with it"
expressions aren't familiar to me' (p. 332), possibly
because McCorquodale has 'learned to accept the irrational in everyday life'. At the end of the play, the
Reverend Pringle, an evangelical huckster who leads The
Brotherhood, is willingly arrested for a murder he has not
committed in order to maintain his reputation as a pious
man who has killed his wife taken in adultery. He is put in
the embarrassing predicament of having to produce the
body when a crime reporter threatens to expose his 'trendy
success' as a murderer. Pringle is being lionised, feted, and
otherwise entertained by romantic ladies who want 'the
privilege of kissing hands that'd taken human life' (p. 344).
Because he cannot risk exposure, he may be forced actually
to do in the wife he has already murdered. Caulfield
explains the dilemma: 'Unless you kill your wife she'll
accuse you of not being her murderer. . . . You're a
clergyman. It's time you practised what you preach' (p.
353).

It is a wonderfully farcical situation, yet *Funeral Games* is
disappointing in its execution. It lacks the intellectual verve
of *Loot*, though it has many splendidly anti-Christian
epigrams. Pringle, for example, scoffs at the central tenets
of Christianity when Caulfield counsels charity:

CAULFIELD: Love thy neighbour.
PRINGLE: The man who said that was crucified by his.
(p. 340)

Or Tessa, Pringle's errant wife, holds up McCorquodale's symbolic watercolour of the Christian Church: 'A bird of prey carrying an olive branch. You've put the matter in a nutshell' (p. 355). But the verbal brilliance in *Funeral Games* stands apart from the dramatic context. The parody murder story is delightful and the anti-religious satire is teasingly provocative, yet the characters remain unrealised. This play is a good demonstration that wit is not enough to energise farce, neither is plot, no matter how complicated. Some compelling dramatic idea, embodied in situation and character, has to make the play work. Orton is too detached and impersonal an observer to make the religious satire effective.

Orton's last play, *What the Butler Saw*, begun in late 1966 and finished by 10 July 1967, was presented posthumously at the Queen's Theatre on 5 March 1969. This was followed by a much better production directed by Lindsay Anderson at the Royal Court Theatre (and later at the Whitehall) on 16 July 1975. *What the Butler Saw* is undoubtedly Orton's comic masterpiece. Although it may have lacked one final revision and could not benefit, as did *Loot*, from the author's prolific rewrites, there is no basis at all for thinking, as John Russell Taylor does, that it is in 'an extremely provisional form' (p. 139). It brings to fruition the kind of anarchic and highly wrought farce that Orton had been writing for his entire career. It is intricately plotted, consistently epigrammatic, and has a cast of sharply drawn, memorable characters both major and minor. Its overt parody of Oscar Wilde's *The Importance of Being Earnest* adds momentum to the farcical/melodrama-

23

tic denouement that proves the steamy incest so wildly postulated by Dr Rance.

What the Butler Saw is, very literally, a sexual farce, but with a much wider range of sexual options than Feydeau could have imagined. Orton's polymorphous perversity liberates a tremendous charge of sexual energy. Mrs Prentice speaks for the play when she demands: 'I want account taken of my sexual nature' (p. 423). Her husband the psychiatrist describes her as a nymphomaniac: 'Consequently, like the Holy Grail, she's ardently sought after by young men' (p. 368). She was born with her legs apart: 'They'll send you to the grave in a Y-shaped coffin' (p. 371). Whom are we to believe and at what moment in the play? All values are relative and fluid, and especially those connected with gender and sexual preference. Mrs Prentice has the illusion that 'The world is full of naked men running in all directions!' (p. 437), but this is also literally true. Presumably the triumphant movement of the farce brings sexual fulfilment for her and for everyone else concerned. The mysterious box with which Geraldine, from the Friendly Faces Employment Bureau, enters the play is discovered to contain the missing phallus of the statue of Sir Winston Churchill, which was found embedded in her step-mother (echoing the apocalyptic ending of *Candy*, published in 1964). At the end of the play Sergeant Match, the triumphant shaman, *'holds high the nation's heritage'* (p. 448), while *'The dying sunlight from the garden and the blaze from above'* gild him with a mysterious halo. Mother, daughter, father and son are ecstatically reunited in the warm glow of fated incest, and all the characters together make a rhapsodic exit: *'They pick up their clothes and weary, bleeding, drugged and drunk, climb the rope ladder into the blazing light'* (p. 448). Orton delighted in these grandiosely illuminated final tableaux. At the end of *The*

24

Erpingham Camp, '*The body of* ERPINGHAM *is left alone in the moonlight with the red balloons and dying flames in a blaze from the distant stained glass*' (p. 320).

The sexual anarchy of *What the Butler Saw* frees the characters from both dogmatism and literalising. Identifications are not hard and fast and permanent, and 'Marriage excuses no one the freaks' roll-call' (p. 409). Madness is liberating in many senses, one of which is that it liberates most of the characters from their clothes. The farce is enacted very simply on the level of costume: the loss of one's clothes, the exchange of clothes, or nakedness as a transitional state. Everyone always seems to be trying out someone else's costume (and therefore identity). In the eyes of the psychiatric inspector-general, Dr Rance, who is the maddest of them all, Dr Prentice is the most typically fluid character in the play: 'As a transvestite, fetishist, bi-sexual murderer Dr. Prentice displays considerable deviation overlap. We may get necrophilia too. As a sort of bonus' (p. 428). Even more than *The Erpingham Camp*, *What the Butler Saw* is frenziedly Dionysiac and Bacchic, its characters enacting various obscene fertility rites. The purpose of Dr Prentice's private sanatorium, as Mrs Prentice so well understands, 'isn't to cure, but to liberate and exploit madness' (p. 388); this is obviously the purpose of Orton's farce.

Everyone gets equal time to do his or her thing without either approbation or moral disapproval. Orton pokes mischievous fun at the homosexual's mystique about heterosexuality in Nick's exchange with Prentice:

NICK: I'm sorry if my behaviour last night caused your wife anxiety, but I've a burning desire to sleep with every woman I meet.

25

Joe Orton

PRENTICE: That's a filthy habit and, in my opinion, very
injurious to the health.

NICK: It is, sir. My health's never been the same since I
went off stamp-collecting. (p. 395)

This is in the festive spirit of Orton's comment on the
relations of Hal and Dennis in *Loot*: 'Americans see
homosexuality in terms of fag and drag. This isn't my vision
of the universal brotherhood. They must be perfectly
ordinary boys who happen to be fucking each other' (Lahr.
p. 205). Orton's satire on heterosexuality is also an attack
on English gentility and the complacent celebration of
middle-class respectability. When Prentice asserts that he is
a heterosexual, Rance protests against the use of sexual
clichés: 'I wish you wouldn't use these Chaucerian words.
It's most confusing' (p. 411). To make any kind of sexual
claim at all suggests the bigotry of a closed mind.

Up Against It, a film script for the Beatles that was never
produced, was the last work that Orton completed before
his death. It was published by Eyre Methuen in 1979. *Up
Against It* was written quickly from about mid-January
1967 to mid-February during the time Orton was still
revising *What the Butler Saw*. On 12 January Walter
Shenson, the producer of two Beatles' movies, *A Hard
Day's Night* and *Help*, got in touch with Orton to re-write a
script for a new Beatles' film. Orton has an elaborate
account of the Beatles episode in his diaries (which are
extensively quoted by Lahr); it is quite clear that the whole
affair was based on a profound misunderstanding of what
Orton represented. Brian Epstein, the Beatles' manager,
wanted a wholesome, clean-cut, but nevertheless far-out
image of his boys for the sanitised drug and pop culture of
middle-class audiences. *Up Against It* was much too
anarchic and comically liberating for the Beatles' commer-

cial interests, and Joe Orton too revolutionary a writer. Obviously no-one in the Beatles entourage had done his homework.

Orton considered the Beatles assignment a lark, and he wrote *Up Against It* in the free and easy, parodic style of *What the Butler Saw*. The tone of *Up Against It* is very different from its source in Orton's ponderous early novel, *Head to Toe*. The film script also draws on the unpublished novel, *The Silver Bucket* (1953), written with Halliwell. Orton claimed that he was plagiarising his early work for the characters in *Up Against It*: 'I shall just do all my box of tricks – Sloane and Hal on them. After all if I repeat myself in this film it doesn't matter. Nobody who sees the film will have seen *Sloane* or *Loot*' (Lahr, p. 243). This is more polite self-deprecation than statement of fact, since *Up Against It* has little to do with *Sloane* or *Loot* but is very much in the quick, dazzling, free-association style of *What the Butler Saw*. Above all in this film Orton seeks a comic impudence and insolence. Romantic clichés of sentimental Hollywood movies are comically exploded. Both of the heroines are conventional Hollywood types: the *'rather plain girl'* (p. 1), Miss Drumgoole, who wins the hero – and his two friends – in the end, and Rowena Torrence, the vamp, who is 'the most modern woman in the world', and who invites Low to 'join her in her "with it" mode of life' (p. 42).

In the frenzied, Dionysiac climax of the film, Ian McTurk, whose heart has been broken by Rowena, finally offers himself to Miss Drumgoole, who has been pursuing him throughout the action: 'My heart is broken, but everything else is in working order. I'd make an excellent husband' (p. 68). The revolutionary Ramsay (full of radical opinions like Tanner in Shaw's *Man and Superman*) delivers a gay diatribe on marriage as the *via media*: 'Getting married and having children is the most rebellious thing a man can do. It shows a disregard for the conventional bourgeois status-quo and a fine, careless anarchic sense of the absurd' (p. 68). Miss Drumgoole is convinced that it is perfectly legal to marry all three musketeers together, an event celebrated with appropriate rapture: '*They hug and kiss her on all parts of her body simultaneously. She gasps for breath and closes her eyes in ecstasy*' (p. 68). This would also be a perfect stage direction for *What the Butler Saw* because it realises Orton's ideal of polymorphous perversity. Miss Drumgoole goes beyond her wildest wish to possess Ian McTurk, since she now has Ian and his friends, and Ramsay, Low and McTurk will never be separated. In the final, ambiguous stage direction, Miss Drumgoole '*squeals with delight and disappears under the coverlet with her husbands*' (p. 70) – who, of course, also disappear with each other. What a wonderful opportunity the Beatles missed to enlarge their repertory – three in male attire and one in drag.

2
Sardonic Intellectualising in 'Head to Toe'

Head to Toe (1971) is Orton's only published novel; it was originally written in 1961 as *The Vision of Gombold Proval*. It is a dream-vision allegory of a journey on the body of a great giant or 'afreet' (a figure from Arabic mythology) from head to toe and back, both on the body and in the body. On the return voyage, the travellers come through the colon and alimentary canal. In the apocalyptic ending, the afreet finally dies and all possibility of continuing the parasitic human existence on its body comes to an end. Gombold disappears down the same hole in the forest with which the novel began, thus establishing its ironic relation to *Alice in Wonderland*.

Is *Head to Toe* a 'crucial text', as Bigsby calls it? I doubt it, although it establishes that peculiar mixture of farce and violence that is characteristic of Orton's later work. It also has a blankness of tone and the acerbic, impersonal, public style of his plays. Bits and pieces of *Head to Toe* are to

29

reappear – the kinky brothel called Consummatum Est (pp. 139ff.) figures in *Loot*, some of the dialogue about clothes and sexual identity on p. 28 is echoed by Dr Rance in *What the Butler Saw*, and the friend who meets a man 'who wanted him to pose for nude photos' (p. 95) comes back again in *Entertaining Mr. Sloane*. The male prostitute with 'a lovely pair of leather jeans', a 'little vest, with the motor oil on his face' is a preliminary sketch for Sloane: 'it's not just sex it's poetry, pure poetry. . . . Anybody can give you sex but the Consummatum Est gives you the poetry of sex at no extra charge' (p. 141).

These verbal links are hardly crucial, yet *Head to Toe* is a teasing catalogue of Orton's themes, images and verbal preoccupations. The novel as a whole is dull and sophomoric. Many of the witty effects do not come off and seem merely decorative and clever. There is an irritating parade of learned allusions throughout, especially to classical mythology and high culture, undoubtedly through the influence of Kenneth Halliwell – perhaps some of the novel was written or rewritten by him. The Trojan Horse episode (pp. 77ff.) comes out of Nathanael West's *Dream Life of Balso Snell* (1931), as Bigsby points out, and the whole mordant and self-conscious novelette serves as a stylistic model for Orton. Like West, Orton is archly pedantic in the Trojan Horse scene, with references to Brutus, great-grandson of Aeneas, and Nennius, who, Gombold thought, 'knew what he was talking about after all' (p. 77). A crude drawing of Helen shows her as an androgynous figure: 'a round face, a button nose, and straight hair, cropped like a boy's' (p. 78). This is hardly the Helen of Renaissance Italian painting. The parody of Death's 'Et in Arcadia ego' ('Et in Suburbia ego', p. 105) certainly sounds like Halliwell at his primly worst, as is Gombold's reaction to the afreet's penis:

It stood up from the ground, bulging and bristling, its walls veined by blue streaks. So vast, so steep, so mighty that it seemed a new world rising out of the old; a world of its own, beautiful and menacing. A vast erection of the earth. Gombold caught his breath as he muttered, 'Suspirum [suspirium?] et decus puellarum et puerorum' [the object of longing and the ornament of girls and boys].   (p. 86)

The learned autodidact, Doktor von Pregnant, Gombold's prison mate, speaks in the authentic voice of Halliwell as spiritual guide and teacher. He introduces the uninformed Gombold to a garbled version of Western Culture:

A slight effort of memory enabled me to recall the contents of many books. I could recite the whole of Shoxbear [Shakespeare], Arrispittle [Aristotle], Grubben [Gibbon?], Taciturn [Tacitus], Saint Trimmer-Ac-Whinous [St Thomas Aquinas], Saint Ginn of the Crutch [St John of the Cross], Goitre [Goethe], Dinty [Dante], and Kneetchur [Nietzsche]. I committed to memory extensive commentaries on Mockbreath [*Macbeth*], King Lour [*King Lear*], the choretricks and egglogres of Furgrill [chorics and eclogues of Virgil] and the Purgreese List of Milltongue [*Paradise Lost* of Milton].   (p. 64)

I quote so extensively because *Head to Toe* is extremely difficult to obtain. With its elementary wordplay, this passage is both exhibitionistic and parodistic, but hardly Joycean in any real sense. Doktor von Pregnant, of course, is a ridiculously ineffectual figure, one of Gombold's 'waking visions' (p. 65), who is fortuitously shot in his prison escape by pursuers going the other way.

Orton delights in the onomastics of *Head to Toe*. There are grand lists of proper names like those he kept in his notebooks. Among the soldiers who visit Gombold's privy-prison,

> Boar, Honour, Speculate and Whitsalt, were the most noticeable. And Dogg [a name Stoppard uses in 'Dogg's *Hamlet*'] the most assured. And Loosefish the most violent. And Crim the most handsome. And Cathole the most intelligent. And Snapturtle, Droop, Propagate, Lill and Rutt, the most quarrelsome. (p. 57)

At the beginning of the novel, when Gombold meets the fat man he rescues from the hole, he wonders 'which minion of his invention this could be'. There is a blurring of imagination and reality as Gombold's characters

> came crowding into his mind: Ballpander, Grendoll, Catsbody and Frag; Olimpicol, Devilday, Wormforce and the Lord of Difference. He remembered Blazon and the incumbent of the Strangler; the man who rode upon a fly and the philosopher Sheenshite. (p. 6)

The names represent a vituperative phonology with certain continuing sounds and images (Catsbody and Cathole). The properties of Sir Shelumiel Cush are more exuberantly named:

> He had recently built and opened, the Sweet Times hotel, All eyes, Wild Manners, the Sentinel, and was thinking of extending the Predator (which had seventy-three exits and five hundred lifts). (p. 80)

The names are surrealistically disquieting.

The characters in the novel have mostly allegorical names, although they are not all easy to decipher. The rich man, Vulp, who has bad teeth 'because if you are rich it does not particularly matter whether you disgust people or not' (p. 7), is vulpine or wolflike. Connie Hogg, the Amazonian Chief of Police, is enormously big and hoglike, and Corporal Squall is the angry man. Gombold Proval (Prove-all) is a Candide-like figure trying to rationalise an irrational reality. What are we to make of the name Gombold? The last syllable is both 'bold' and 'balled', and the first suggests 'gum'. Is 'gumballed' a possible phonetic link with Gombold as an anonymous and mechanistic product of the gum-ball machine? He is certainly a character of ambiguous masculinity.

The foolishly theoretical and impractical Offjenkin, who appears twice, seems obviously to play on 'offjerking' or 'jerking off'. He is the onanistic anti-hero. One of the books that O'Scullion buys is *Onanie in der Pubertäte* (p. 94), and Gombold conceives of the imagination in masturbatory terms: 'Was it possible to create oneself a kind of phantom Gombold from the void of onanistic satisfaction? This creature was nothing but a spurt of mental fluid' (p. 14). Offjenkin is supremely a creation of 'mental fluid'. He is lost in a world of pointless gestures and words. His terrorist activities are in the histrionic style of Monty Python's Flying Circus:

> he circulated among a crowd of women in a restaurant and told them the proprietor was mad; he organised a march into the city centre wearing a mask and carrying a banner on which nothing was written. . . .   (p. 147)

An empty banner is the ultimate political message.

33

Joe Orton

Offjenkin exerts a tremendous influence on Gombold, especially in the area of explosive words. The passages from pp. 144–50 are those that critics of Orton quote most frequently from *Head to Toe*, as if they presaged his special theory of language as weapon. In context, however, the statements are much more parodistic than doctrinal. Offjenkin is the most Alice-in-Wonderland character in the novel; he believes in the magical reality of words for their own sake – words as autonomous, self-explaining gestures. He and his men have a charmingly pointless but rigid set of values:

> 'We are against fragments, wonderful ventures, allegorical dramas, sentences more than eight words long, second chances, old men with green eyes, chinese-white, murder without crime, miracles, text-books on Hygiene, muscle re-education and all forms of stammering', said Offjenkin.
>   A man nearby cleaning a machine gun said, 'And phonology.'
>   'And young men with four shirts and choice silver wedding presents,' said another.   (p. 144)

This is Orton at his farcical best; we think immediately of the capriciously pithy nonsense of *What the Butler Saw*. Of course playwrights are against stammering and machine-gunners are opposed to phonology, but why 'chinese-white?' This figures into the decorator's scheme for Molly's house: 'She's going to have it re-decorated in Chinese white lacquer and natural oak woodwork' (p. 37).

Offjenkin is equally vehement in declaring his positive ideology:

> 'We are in favour of walls,' he said, 'and Norse folk

34

tales, "I love you", dream houses, spider's webs, village greens, cuckoldry within reason, psychoanalytical studies of Hamlet, domestic bliss, first hand information and cross-stitching.'

The man nearby cleaning the machine gun said, 'And beginner's luck.'

'And clowns, wisdom teeth, dead roses and mouse-traps,' said another.   (p. 144)

This is a rather pre-Raphaelite catalogue, in which the items eventually seem less incongruous than at first sight. Psychoanalytical studies of Hamlet are a form of literary cross-stitching, and beginner's luck comes to those who say 'I love you' and read Norse folk tales. Anyone who loves dead roses and mousetraps can hardly be terrifying to the enemy.

It is against this background that Gombold develops his theory of words:

> Gombold realised that the tactics they were using had proved useless. Words were more effective than actions; in the right hand verbs and nouns could create panic. Offjenkin had made an attempt to design a sentence which would speak for itself, but had abandoned the idea as too destructive.   (p. 148)

I think Orton is using the word 'panic' in a special, socially conscious way. It is the effect of disturbing middle-class, genteel values, turning the audience inside out, as Orton had in mind for *What the Butler Saw*. He saw the need to 'hot up' the play when he rewrote it, 'Sex is the only way to infuriate them. Much more fucking and they'll be screaming hysterics in next to no time.'[1]

Thus Gombold studies words as the secret weapon:

The war was a few weeks old when he started to construct the perfect sentence. Squall allowed him a tent to himself, and he studied the chemistry and behaviour of words, phrase design, the forging, casting and milling, the theories of paraphrase and periphrase, the fusing and the aiming.

In a library he unearthed accounts of the damage words had done in the past. His figures showed that when a particularly dangerous collection of words exploded the shock waves were capable of killing centuries after-wards. (p. 149)

The war is a ridiculous and pointless enterprise without ideology, so that Gombold is merely experimenting in the arts of punishing rhetoric. The whole passage is Orton's most extended statement of what Handke calls 'offending the audience'.

We are not surprised to learn that the written word is less effective than the spoken word:

To be destructive, words had to be irrefutable. And then the book might not be read. He was aware that words and sentences often buried themselves into readers' minds before exploding and then went off harmlessly. Print was less effective than the spoken word because the blast was greater; eyes could ignore, slide past, dangerous verbs or nouns. But if you could lock the enemy into a room somewhere and fire the sentence at them you would get a sort of seismic disturbance. . . . (p. 149)

The 'room', of course, is the theatre, and the passage makes a nice allegory if we see in it Orton's farewell to the novel and the assertion of his new commitment to the theatre. But this is to ignore Orton's subtle playfulness and distaste

for manifestos and dogma. Both Offjenkin and Gombold
are hopelessly emasculated figures, Walter Mittys and
Caspar Milquetoasts, whose inflamed fantasies are purely
compensatory. Even Gombold's much quoted prayer,
'Mother, cleanse my heart, give me the ability to rage
correctly' (p. 61), is part of his effort, enclosed in a privy,
to survey the world, and it concludes with the not too
elevating thought, 'Let me learn why Prudence begins with
a P' (a possible pun on the pee of Gombold's situation). It is
quite possible that the emphasis should fall on raging
correctly, as if the ritual and gesture must be correct in
order to be effective.

In typical Orton fashion there is a great deal of
polymorphous perversity in *Head to Toe*. The sexes are
confused, and sexual identity is as floating and ambiguous
an area as personal identity: Gombold is the passive
observer of the flotsam and jetsam of historic events,
alternating methodically between being a revolutionary
and a prisoner. He seems to project the images of reality, in
onanistic fashion, on the screen of his own mind. In his
travels Gombold comes upon a city in which the inhabitants

> exhibited rhythmical consecutive sexuality. In all cases
> the initial sex was male, followed by a series of alternat-
> ing female and male phases throughout life. As a rule the
> adult completed one male and one female phase every
> five years, but in some cases individuals had as many as
> three changes of sex, with a period of hermaphroditism,
> during that time. In addition the population contained a
> number of true males who retained the male phase
> indefinitely.   (p. 91)

Gombold adds significantly: 'they were a happy people'.
Rhythmical consecutive sexuality allows for a wider range

of possibilities than a hard and fast sexual identity. Thus Gombold can stay loose without being oppressively either male or female.

Early in the novel, when Gombold becomes the kept man of Connie Hogg, the enormous Chief of Police, we see the reversal of sexual identity in its most vivid form. In this society women rule. The Amazonian leaders are masculinised in all respects except that they remain intensely and caricaturally feminine in their concern for clothes and interior decoration. Gombold is feminised by his powerfully masculine mistress, who takes him prisoner. Although he is forbidden to 'wear Daddy's clothes' (p. 20). Gombold cannot resist his transvestite urges:

> The urge became stronger when he brushed the tweed of her coats, or ironed the linen of her shirts. Power resided in her clothes: if he wore her clothes he could become powerful like her.   (p. 20)

Gombold is made to suffer for being 'a wicked little bitch' (p. 25). When he returns he is severely punished for venturing out as a man; he is both feminised and infantilised. ' "Are you out of your mind?" says the disbelieving Connie. "This is your bedroom. Is it a man's room?" She switched on the light; Gombold blinked. It was a pretty, frilly, pinky room. "No man would have a room like this. You are a woman" ' (p. 26). The dialogue sounds like *Entertaining Mr. Sloane*, where Kath mothers – and smothers in peremptory affection – the errant but compliant Sloane. Gombold capitulates completely to Connie: 'Strong arms enfolded him. He was safe. However difficult it might be he would never disobey her again' (p. 27).

Gombold's ambiguous and fluid sexuality is only one among many homosexual touches in *Head to Toe*. The most obvious one is the fascination with and fear of women, especially phallic women like Connie and Lilly, the Prime Minister. It is not surprising that the novel turns on the assassination of the Prime Minister by Gombold and the subsequent shaking of gynaecocracy. Immediately following the assassination, the mood of the female mob turns ugly and homicidal as a nameless delivery man is lynched in a style reminiscent of Cinna the Poet in Shakespeare's *Julius Caesar*:

> In the forecourt of the building and in the nearby streets there were many who believed that it was an anonymous male crime, committed not by a man but by Man. And presently some of the women with revenge in their hearts began to canvass about for a male to crucify.   (p. 42)

The women make animal noises as they close in on the innocent delivery man:

> he heard their voices now only as myriad and interminable insects. Falling into the gutter, breathing the sickening smell of blood, thinking how when he was younger, a boy, a youth, he had loved the sight of female flesh and the sound of women's voices, of walking or sitting alone with them under trees. He never knew the danger. Then the pavement, the stones, became actual, savage, filled with, evocative of, the claws of birds, maddening, terrifying sounds. He was afraid.
> And then he died.   (p. 43)

The sexuality evoked is that of a boy's voyeuristic love of 'the sight of female flesh and the sound of women's voices'. We recall the poem of Gombold lying in his coffin, which begins, 'Let us murder our mothers . . .' (p. 61).

In his privy-prison, Gombold studies, like Shake-speare's Richard II, 'how he might liken this house of ordure to the world' (p. 55). The poem written on toilet paper that he slips under his stall in a mute appeal to rescue a 'young writer', is shadowy in the area of object-love. There is, in fact, a deliberate blurring of subject and object, male and female:

> I am the girl's delight,
> I am the stallion.
> (I am the girls I myself have enjoyed.)   (p. 56)

Earlier he was 'the speckled white cock's/Desire for hens'. In the burlesque discourse of the tricksy Doktor von Pregnant, he explains the mysteries from Thomas Browne's *Religio Medici*: 'As for the name Achilles assumed – PHYLLIS. Little Phyllis they called him. And everyone knew he was a boy' (p. 67).

Gombold the assassin of women: this is the crucial event of the narrative and one that makes him a revolutionary fugitive. But the context of Lilly, the Prime Minister's, murder is the exceptionally trivial chit-chat about fashions and interior design. Although the women rule, they make no attempt to engage in macho conversation. Instead, they are intensely, cattily, bitchily domestic. Affairs of state are bathetically reduced to affairs of the hemline and chic textiles. The press conference with the Prime Minister shows Orton at his most vivacious, with a wonderful ear for fatuous detail:

> 'Are you in favour of direct contact with our rivals?'
> 'In certain circumstances I am. Though after the disgraceful things they said about my drawing-room

curtains last time, I don't think I can make too great an
effort to be polite.'

'But Lillian, that would be fatal.'

'They were the latest screen-printed furnishing fab-
rics: matt-black with an azalea motif.'   (pp. 37–8)

This homosexual camp does not explain why Gombold has
to shoot Lillian, but no other reason is ever given. It is
obvious that Gombold both delights in the world of women
and is terrified by it.

Head to Toe is a very self-conscious novel, which at times
plays on its own satirical self-awareness of its self-
consciousness. In Chapter Ten, Gombold pretends to be the
lionised author whom the seventy-seven women and two
men meeting to discuss his work suddenly invite to lunch.
The author is a great popular success and an exact antitype
to Orton: 'he evokes a scene beautifully, such a stringent eye
for character' (p. 101). Orton is making fun of his own novel,
in which the characters (as well as the sexes) are more or
less interchangeable and no scenes are evoked at all. There
is a blizzard of literary chit-chat just before Gombold
appears: 'I think one may observe in the best of his work a
close relationship between the state of contemplative
awareness and the intellectual attraction for pure dialectic'
(p. 101). Orton seems to be mocking Beckett, and
especially *Waiting for Godot*, in this parody of public
profundity: 'Kemmerling has interpreted the work in a
platonic sense. Henpate thinks it is a symbol of the
unconscious' (p. 99). The work that Gombold extem-
poraneously composes for his admirers is a spoof of a
children's story about old aunt Bear and uncle Bear going
about their chores '*In the ruins of the British Museum*' (p.
101). Old aunt Bear '*was a good Bear, but not a happy one*',

to whom Frances O'Malley Whipsnade Polar makes a kinky suggestion: ' "*My Dear*", *she said*, "*what you need is a good blow. To take you out of yourself*" ' (p. 102). It is at this point that the hostess, Jenny, exposes Gombold as a fraud.

What does it mean to be an author? This was a question that interested Orton and Halliwell intensely, since they had given up their rather mediocre careers as actors and were now full-time authors. It is clear that Orton is laughing at himself through the eyes of Gombold, and this is certainly one of the saving graces of *Head to Toe*. If it is bizarre and unfocused as a novel, it is also full of wonderfully comic touches. Thus Gombold, in a frantic effort to escape from his privy-prison, experiments in a new genre:

> One day Gombold made a paper dart of another poem: it was the kind of writing he had never done before, indeed he was convinced it was of a type no one had ever attempted in any language. (p. 57)

This has a rather mock-heroic cast; Gombold's dart-poems are returned unopened. But suddenly the rather humdrum prose comes alive as it is converted into dramatic dialogue:

> Then he heard a voice say, 'You in there.'
> Gombold looked up. An eye was pressed to the hole in the door.
> 'What?' Gombold asked.
> 'Stop writing poems.'
> 'I have to pass the time away.'
> 'There are other ways. I'm not picking up your muck every time I pass.'
> 'Who are you?'

> 'My name's Squall. I'm a corporal in charge of
> ablutions.' (p. 57)

The conflict between author and public is neatly joined,
with Orton strongly aware of the disabilities and pretensions on both sides. Squall is obviously reading the
prisoner's poems, since he knows they are poems as well as
muck. Orton and Gombold did not need to be heavily
persuaded in order to follow Squall's sound advice: 'Stop
writing poems'.

Once Squall disappears from the prison, Gombold turns
in upon his own imagination, and the 'odd fantasies (p. 59)
that follow are an inventory of a writer's resources:
'Gradually he turned from life and lowered himself, as in a
diving bell, plumbing the ocean of mystic contemplation'
(p. 60). The flood of images shows Gombold how to write
Head to Toe: 'By use of images it might be possible to
extract from fantasy a kind of reality' (p. 60). Although the
imagery is somewhat cute and fanciful, it offers a model for
the writer to be true to his own experience:

> Gombold, the prisoner, imprisoning reason, experi-
> enced an opening of windows, a smashing of barriers,
> and a cleansing. Saw again his wanderings. Saw the
> animals in the forest; wheels, springs and coils of sense
> and nonsense. He had succeeded in breaking down the
> walls so that his experience recorded clear and true, in its
> totality, was not a single unit, but many separate units,
> melting and fusing into a vision. (p. 61)

This is the significance of Orton's title, *The Vision of
Gombold Proval*. The passage is strangely prophetic of
Orton's own six-month term in prison for defacing library
books and the invigorating effect it had on his own writing.
The clarification seems to come through imprisoning

reason, a way of working out one's irrational, impulsive and unconscious imagery. This is the cleansing process, and it is significant that the whole passage immediately follows Orton's much quoted injunction: 'Mother, cleanse my heart, give me the ability to rage correctly' (p. 61). Perhaps the ability to rage correctly comes from the ability to smash barriers, open windows, and break down walls (in the imagery of the passage). Through a violent wrenching of reason comes the purified vision of how to write farce.

3
Stylistic Experiments: 'The Ruffian on the Stair', 'Funeral Games', 'Until She Screams'

I have put together two short plays by Orton, *The Ruffian on the Stair* and *Funeral Games*, and the brief sketch, *Until She Screams*, because all three are stylistic experiments that are not entirely successful. It might be useful to consider what went wrong in each of these attempts. *The Ruffian on the Stair*, written in 1963 and broadcast on the BBC Third Programme in 1964, was Orton's first performed work. *Funeral Games* dates from 1966, between *Loot* (1964–6) and *What the Butler Saw* (1967) – in other words, at the height of Orton's career. *Until She Screams*, published in *Evergreen Review* in 1970, is a very slight pornographic skit, lightly revised from *The Patient Dowager* of 1960.

In *The Ruffian on the Stair* Orton was still working out his relation to Pinter. Mike, the hired killer, seems to come right out of the pages of Pinter's *Dumb Waiter* (written in 1957),[1] where all the factual details are kept at a distance and only occasionally filter through the dense thickets of irrelevant allusions. Mike's comings and goings are difficult to trace. The play begins with his appointment 'at King's Cross station at eleven. I'm meeting a man in the toilet' (p. 31), to which Joyce has an un-Pinteresquely farcical rejoinder: 'You always go to such interesting places'. Later Mike is 'seeing a man who could put me in touch with something' (p. 43), which, in its portentous vagueness, sounds like a take-off on Pinter. Mike's speech at the beginning of Scene 2 is entirely characteristic of his Pinteresque origins:

> I went to the King's Cross toilet like I told you. I met my contact. He was a man with bad feet. He looked as though life had treated him rough. He hadn't much to live for. I gave him the message from the – er – (*Pause.*) The message was delivered. I went outside on the platform. It was cold. I saw an old girl hardly able to breathe. Had something wrong with her. Hardly able to breathe. Her face was blue. (*Pause.*) Are you listening, Joycie?   (p. 37)

The shadowiness of the man with bad feet and the woman who is hardly able to breathe is inconsequential rather than menacing, and the whole speech sounds like a bad imitation of Pinter, complete with pregnant repetitions and pauses and the withholding of crucial information. We do not need this significant speech for the development of Mike's character.

Similarly, the place-names that punctuate the dialogue of Mike and Wilson later in the play are very much in the style of Pinter but not of any real consequence. They occur almost as a stylistic tic:

> WILSON: I've walked all the way from the bus station by Victoria. Do you know that district at all?
> MIKE: I know King's Cross intimately.
> WILSON: Victoria is a different place entirely. In the summer it has a character of its own. (p. 45)

We know about Mike's association with King's Cross, but Victoria Station has no bearing on the suicidal Wilson. Mike feels sympathy for Wilson's part-Irish background and wants to establish points of contact:

> MIKE: What part of Ireland is your mother from?
> WILSON: Sligo.
> MIKE: I once knew a lad from Sligo. Name of Murphy. I wonder if maybe your Ma would've come across him?
> WILSON: I'll make enquiries.
> MIKE: I'd be obliged if you would. He had dark curly hair and talked with a pronounced brogue. Not an easy man to miss in a crowd. (p. 46)

Nothing further is heard of Murphy, and Wilson's mother assumes a role in the dialogue out of all proportion to her intrinsic interest. Everything is properly dislocated and displaced in the style of Pinter, so that the audience is rendered more than a little uneasy at the irrelevance of what is being said, but this type of dialogue works against the farcical and epigrammatic style that was to become Orton's most characteristic achievement. In *The Ruffian on the Stair* the two styles are uncomfortably juxtaposed.

On the opposite side of the stylistic equation, Wilson

taunts Mike with his cuckoldry in a slangy, syncopated, irritating tone distinctly different from Pinter:[2]

> I might decide to put Maddy in the pudding club. Just to show my contempt for your way of life. I never take precautions. We're skin to skin. Nature's method.
>
> (p. 54)

Mike fears the young Wilson's virility; he himself is no longer able to enrol his wife in the 'pudding club' (make her pregnant). Mike's soliloquy after the taunting Wilson exits is both ridiculous and touching in a combination typical of Orton: 'They think because you're a criminal they can treat you like dirt. Coming here like that. Telling a man to his face. The morals of Nineveh were hardly so lax' (p. 54). The speech seems to be put together from vaudeville one-liners (criminals being treated without respect), learned allusions (the Nineveh of the *Book of Jonah*), and personal pain (confronting the cuckold with his own inadequacy). The range of Mike's soliloquy is much more Shakespearean and Jacobean than anything in Pinter. Mike is full of self-pity and manly revenge: 'I've a clear case. I'm the injured party. I'll have the stones off him if he's done her' (p. 55). The sexual language is all directly macho – or rather it is an attempt to assert the macho values that the cuckold believes are being called in question.

Everything is mixed and contradictory in this soliloquy, but there is no menacing vagueness of allusion. The speech is up front and we are made to feel compassion for the foolish Mike's dilemma. His Joyce has had a long and distinguished career as a whore: 'Before I met her she was known to the Directory of Directors as Madelein Scott-Palmer. And before that she'd led a loose life as Sarah Fielding. She wasted her auntie's legacy on cards for tobacconists' windows' (p. 55). These are presumably the euphemistic advertisements that one sees in Soho for French lessons (discipline strictly enforced), water sports, dog-walking, etc. The extravagant details and the stiff and stilted style culminate in Mike's decision not to kill Joyce: 'She's all I've got. I want her if she's the biggest old tart since the mother of Solomon.' The allusion to traditions of the Apocrypha about King Solomon's mother is folksy, and the climax of Mike's soliloquy is a perfect Archie Bunker-ism: 'What a life it is living in a country full of whores and communists.'

In this soliloquy Orton clearly separates himself from Pinter by a grotesquely colloquial, non-allusive and non-poetic style. The farcical self-indulgences are deliciously irrelevant, but not in the fashion of Pinter because they tend to humanise the play, reducing its mysterious menace and making Mike a believable character. Nothing in *Ruffian on the Stair* is more comically outrageous than Wilson's explanation of how his dead brother happened to be involved with Maddy: 'He had it off with you after seeing *The Sound of Music*. I waited downstairs. He was as pissed as a fart. He would never have had a prostitute and seen *The Sound of Music* otherwise' (p. 58). This is the sort of wild, off the wall, free-associational detail that Pinter admired in Orton and that clearly separates the two dramatists. Only someone 'as pissed as a fart' – as drunk as a clam? – could have found erotic stimulation in the meanderings of the Trapp family singers.

Funeral Games is a surprisingly unsuccessful play. It was first presented on Yorkshire Television on 25 August 1968, but has had no major theatrical production. Written in a lively, witty style in the period just before *What the Butler Saw*, the play is consistently entertaining, even brilliant, yet the religious satire on which it is based is both sterile and forbidding. All of Orton's plays, and especially *The Erpingham Camp*, make fun of organised religion as an institution that controls and stultifies individuality and spontaneity, but in *Funeral Games* religious chicanery is the main subject and this creates problems. Both the aggressively evangelical Pringle and the defrocked priest McCorquodale are cardboard characters who never come alive. Their particular madness is not energised by any larger vision of human society, as it is, for example, in the psychiatrist Rance in *What the Butler Saw*, who manages to impose his madness on all the other characters. In *Funeral Games*, however, the main characters are remarkably passive and uninvolved. The farcical point of whether Pringle and McCorquodale have murdered their wives – one has, the other has not – and can either produce the *corpus delicti*, or significant parts of it, remains a technicality. By the end of the play we cease to delight in the zany complications by which farce usually engages us. Only the young and unscrupulous private eye. Caulfield, like Hal and Dennis in *Loot*, captivates our interest, especially in his attempt at blackmail: to be 'Taken on to God's payroll' (p. 359).

There is good fun in *Funeral Games* but it is detached from the action and presents itself more in the form of gags, epigrams and routines than in some meaningful relation to character and story. Scene 6 is especially rich in comic material. One typical example of a grotesque, interpolated story is the account of the snake by Tessa, Pringle's wife. She has abandoned her husband in order to look after McCorquodale, who is lonely partly because he has murdered his own wife, Valerie, Tessa's good friend. While Tessa, McCorquodale and Caulfield are having tea, and after Caulfield has hidden the severed hand of Valerie in the cake tin, Tessa announces that 'The young woman by the bridge has left her husband' (p. 348). It seems that the wife was expecting a gift from him but was not prepared for a snake. 'Rows over a snake. . . . She was looking forward to a rabbit or a guinea-pig. Something for baby to play with. . . . Then he tells her he's put a deposit on a five-feet-long python. . . . She was horrified. . . . Isn't it wicked, though, allowing a snake to jeopardize your marriage?' (pp. 348–9). Or your play? Except for its phallic implications, this story is genuinely puzzling. It is told right in the midst of a macabre tea ceremony to which it has no relation except as idle chit-chat.

The humour of Scene 6 is more typically jokey, especially in its use of deflating non-sequiturs, as in the following:

MCCORQUODALE: Questions are being asked about your murder.

TESSA: I never think about it now.

MCCORQUODALE: You were upset at first though, weren't you?

TESSA: Well, nobody likes to be done in. It stands to reason.

(p. 347)

Tessa's final retort is obviously the punch-line to which everything has been leading. The dialogue becomes the occasion for puns and wordplay that are sparked off as if the language were autonomous. When Caulfield complains that he could not get Valerie's head off – 'It must be glued on' (p. 347) – McCorquodale quips: 'She was always a headstrong woman' (p. 348). When Tessa threatens, 'I shall take my troubles to the Police', Caulfield retorts: 'Haven't they got enough of their own?' (p. 349).

McCorquodale's miraculous explanation of Valerie's death, 'She was taken up to Heaven. In a fiery chariot. Driven by an angel', is bathetically exploded by Tessa: 'What nonsense! Valerie would never accept a lift from a stranger' (p. 351). The string of gags in Scene 6 gives it a surrealistic tone. We are not meant to believe in the Grand Guignol horrors, but we also cannot forget them. *What the Butler Saw* has the same sort of farcical routines, but the plot has an urgency and feeling of acceleration that is missing from the relaxed and leisurely *Funeral Games*, whose comedy lacks propulsion.

Despite the macabre merriness of *Funeral Games*, its attack on religion is violent in a way that the tone can hardly sustain. Pringle is a shameless, fornicating huckster of The Brotherhood: 'We've a house of contemplation, in the Arcade. . . . We hang about on street corners' (p. 323). The ex-priest McCorquodale, who wishes to God he could commit the sin of adultery he is accused of, is an avowed wife-murderer whose late Valerie is buried in the basement 'under a ton of smokeless coal' (p. 331). He is also identified by a series of Nazi allusions: 'My pictures of dizzy youth in pre-war Berlin. . . . those off-colour snaps of Frau Goebbels. . . . They'd make any man glad he wasn't a Semite' (p. 329). In sum, Pringle and McCorquodale are both thoroughly disagreeable characters. Their nastiness works against the comic effect.

Pringle's viciousness makes him an incongruous figure in farce, and this may be one of the stylistic and generic difficulties of *Funeral Games*. Unlike Erpingham and Rance and Truscott and Mrs Vealfoy, the 'villains' in *Funeral Games* are not attractive. Pringle's assault on Christian charity is not funny because Pringle as a dramatic character lacks the ironic dimension and naughty, self-conscious cleverness of Orton's bad guys. It is not so much the content of his speeches as his smugness that defeats him. At the end of Scene 3, Pringle exits firing his gun and uttering a war cry: 'The humble and the meek are thirsting for blood' (p. 337). This is decidedly anti-Christian but Pringle has never been identified with the humble and the meek, nor has anyone in this play, even Valerie's blind father who cares for the donkeys. Pringle is so much the activist, militant Christian that when Caulfield suggests blackmail, the preacher stops him in his tracks: 'We're Children of Light. Not criminals. Tangle with the Prince of Peace and you'll find a knife in your back' (p. 359).

McCorquodale is a much milder churchman than Pringle, but his valetudinarian impotence more or less undercuts his role in the play. He once saw a vision of the Virgin: 'She wore a floppy hat and had a sweet smile' (p. 327), and he seems sentimentally inclined to the sins of the flesh. The disgrace that led to his being defrocked occurred while he was walking arm in arm with a couple of nuns outside the basilica of St Peter. A mendicant monk objected to something he said and 'Made a terrible mess of my face with his crucifix' (p. 328). Again, there is a violence in the religious allusions that does not properly serve the needs of farce, in which murder itself is never either reprehensible or believable. McCorquodale may have 'learned to accept the irrational in everyday life' (p. 332), but he is still hoping for divine intervention. When Tessa at the end appeals to his manhood: 'Shall I be your wife in name only?', McCorquodale replies: 'Unless a miracle occurs' (p. 358). This is more satisfyingly witty than Orton's rabidly anti-Christian sentiments.

Orton was clearly trying out in *Funeral Games* the kind of exuberant farce that works so well in *What the Butler Saw*. The business with the dead Valerie's hand has comic possibilities that are never fully exploited. Pringle needs to maintain his thrilling but undeserved reputation as a wife-killer. He has received a whole series of valuable gifts from female admirers that he does not want to return: 'This was a present from a woman journalist. She wanted the privilege of kissing hands that'd taken human life. It's so rare in her circle' (p. 344). But Pringle is being pursued by a crime reporter named Paterson, who 'claims your trendy success is a fraud. . . . He's calling on you for proof' (p. 345). The clergyman is put in the embarrassing predicament of having to produce evidence of his guilt: 'Where could I get a human head? Even Harrods wouldn't accept the order' (p. 346).

As go-between and factotum, Caulfield knows where to find a female corpse in McCorquodale's coal pile. In Scene 6 he enters carrying *'a meat cleaver and a human hand, severed above the wrist, wrapped in sacking'* (p. 347). Valerie's supposed hand is the farcical focus of this scene. Caulfield goes to the sink and *'washes the hand and his own'* (p. 348). He puts it in a Dundee cake tin that is conveniently available, but Tessa needs the tin to put away the tea cake. The plot thickens:

TESSA: (*Gasping with fright.*) It's real.
MCCORQUODALE: Plastic.
TESSA: It's real. (*Trembling.*) I can spot plastic fingers a mile off. (p. 350)

In the denouement, Caulfield opens the cake tin and lifts out a human hand as Tessa *'draws a horrified breath'* (p. 359). The sleuth then *'breaks off a finger with a sharp crack'*: 'This isn't a real hand. It's a fake.' Thus everyone is satisfied and Pringle readily confesses to the police a murder he has not committed, while the real murderer,

McCorquodale, chortles merrily: 'Shame. Shame. It'll be banner headlines. The daughters of the Philistines will rejoice' (p. 360). The manic ending of *Funeral Games* resembles *Loot* in its cheerful cynicism. It is a pity that the energies generated by the farcical plot could not have started percolating earlier and that Pringle and McCorquodale are such indistinct characters. The funeral games the title promises never really feel like games until the end. In this sense *Loot* did it all much better before, and the professionalising and literalising of religious cant in *Funeral Games* tends to work against the macabre humour.

Not much need be said about the mildly pornographic sketch, *Until She Screams*, which is very early work (around 1960) heated up for the commercial and show biz eroticism of *Oh! Calcutta!* Orton is attempting a little comedy of manners in the style of Restoration comedy and Oscar Wilde. Lady Shane resembles Lady Wishfort in Congreve's *Way of the World* and Lady Bracknell in *The Importance of Being Earnest*, if we can imagine those imperious ladies as having been without sex for a very long time. No one has 'interfered' with Lady Shane since she was two, 'Except my old English sheepdog'.[3] Later, auntie is again reported not to have had 'a good shag' since she was two: 'Not since the time I was taken aboard the *Victory* and fingered by the ratings. And then soundly done by the Captain' (p. 52). It was a splendid experience, but, as Lady Shane sensibly explains, 'not enough to last me for a lifetime'. Charles's observation that Lady Shane 'must have sawdust up to her navel' is echoed in Ed's misogynistic diatribe against his sister Kath in *Entertaining Mr. Sloane*, but the whole sketch is not of much consequence. The sexual imagination is generally adolescent. The butler O'Dwyer has a usefully radioactive penis and Charles is turned on by talk of flagellation: 'he would work himself up into such a state that if nobody was around he'd meddle with that aspidistra' (p. 52). Lady Shane is the only even vaguely developed character. Her best moment is when she catches fire and begins smoking from under her expensive gown. Mrs Terrington warns her aunt not to relieve herself with 'cardboard phalluses. I always told you the *Daily Sketch* was highly inflammable' (p. 53). The masturbatory qualities of other publications are discussed – the *Lady's Friend*, the *Illustrated London News*, *Peg's Paper* – but 'None of them has the correct pliancy and verve' (p. 51). There is little in this tepid skit that suggests the bold farces that Orton would be writing in the next three or four years.

4
Authority and Entertainment in 'The Good and Faithful Servant' and 'The Erpingham Camp'

The comic villains in Orton are always authority figures: Dr Rance, the inspecting psychiatrist in *What the Butler Saw*, Inspector Truscott of Scotland Yard in *Loot*, the insinuating brother Ed in *Entertaining Mr. Sloane*, the officious and ceremonious Erpingham in *The Erpingham Camp*, and the effusive Mrs Vealfoy from Personnel, who represents the values of the factory. 'Villain' is, of course, the wrong word. There are no villains in Orton even though his farce is often just the other side of melodrama – the merry side turned up by the ingenious and outrageous plotting common to farce and melodrama. Orton's villains are always grotesque comic manipulators, Vice figures who represent the cap-

57

ricious but all-powerful institutions of our society. They are company men and women, like Erpingham and Mrs Vealfoy, who mechanise, regiment, institutionalise and bureaucratise all the functions of human life including pleasure.

The epigraphs to *The Good and Faithful Servant* include not only the eponymous quotation from Matthew 25:21: 'Well done, thou good and faithful servant', but also a dictionary definition of *Faith* from the *Concise Oxford Dictionary*: 'Reliance, trust, *in*; belief founded on authority'. The authority figures in Orton are those we are expected to have faith *in*. They command an automatic response of trust and reliance that forms the basis for Orton's satire. They are the false fathers who chaperone the dominant values of our society.

In a telling essay with Marxist implications, Simon Shepherd lays out Orton's indictment of British society under the rubric of the 'dialectic of entertainment'. Entertainment, especially in its Roman sense of bread and circuses, is a form of social control, and Orton echoes anti-totalitarian, dystopian literature like *1984* and *Brave New World*. In the Erpingham Camp, the Entertainments Organiser is a crucial office, which Chief Redcoat Riley may have killed to attain. In other plays violence is often cloaked in entertainment – was Orton thinking of John Osborne's *The Entertainer* (1957)?[1] – most notably in *Loot*, where Inspector Truscott is the wily, shape-changing and dangerous trickster of folklore. As Shepherd understands so clearly, Orton is using the dialectic of entertainment to attack institutions: the Church, the State, the Factory, Marriage, Pleasure, Mental Health.

Both *The Good and Faithful Servant* and *The Erpingham Camp* were originally television plays presented by Rediffusion, the former in 1967, the latter in 1966, although *The*

Good and Faithful Servant was written in 1964, a year before *The Erpingham Camp*. *The Good and Faithful Servant* is the most direct and most compassionate play that Orton ever wrote, with its protagonist Buchanan closely modelled on his own father. The harshness of the social indictment in this play is only partly mitigated by wit, whereas *The Erpingham Camp* is thoroughly mythologised and displaced. Real life generally served Orton well as material for drama, but he needed a way of converting his own bitter, lower-class experience in Leicester and London as actor, writer, and homosexual into sardonic, gag-like, detached and eloquent comedy. In other words, he needed to farcicalise the very vivid experience on which the plays were based.

Mrs Vealfoy is therefore a much more successful figure in *The Good and Faithful Servant* than the pathetic Buchanan and his aged but recently discovered wife Edith. Above all, Mrs Vealfoy is a cheery person in the style of Dickens. Her mindless but never flagging optimism and good spirits are part of the corporate image of the nameless factory she represents. This factory, of course, functions as a microcosm of British society in much the same way as Erpingham's holiday camp – both plays are intensely political. Mrs Vealfoy is an exemplar of everything British and is therefore another of Orton's remarkable anticipations of Britain in the 1980s. The Director of Personnel officiously arranges Buchanan's retirement ceremony, which is tawdry but correct in every detail. The social tone and class values are immediately established in the first exchange:

MRS VEALFOY: May we be completely informal and call you 'George'?
BUCHANAN: By all means.

MRS VEALFOY: Good, good. (*Laughs*.) My name is Mrs
    Vealfoy.   (pp. 156–7)

We never learn Mrs Vealfoy's first name, although we may
suspect that the family name derives from Defoe's 'True
Relation of the Apparition of one Mrs. Veal' (1706). Was
Orton thinking of French, Anglo-Norman etymologies:
'vielle foi' (old faith) or 'vrai foi' (true faith), meanings that
fit well with the ceremoniousness of the character?

Mrs Vealfoy is incapable of considering Buchanan as a
human being. In her eyes he is a completely mechanised
and bureaucratised non-person. When Buchanan inadver-
tently reveals that he has a newly discovered grandson who
he hopes will come into the firm 'To carry on the tradition'
(p. 158), Mrs Vealfoy is genuinely perturbed: 'Pay atten-
tion to me! What grandson? You've no descendants living.
I have the information from our records' (p. 159). She
accuses the abashed Buchanan of 'feeding false information into our computers'. Buchanan's feeble protest, 'It's a
personal matter. My private life is involved', is easily
answered: 'Should your private life be involved, we shall be
the first to inform you of the fact' (p. 159). Once revealed,
the grandson Ray becomes an immediate candidate for
recruitment into the corporation.

The retirement ceremony in Scene 3 is full of empty,
formulaic language that marks the deadness and meaning-
lessness of the occasion. No one knows or cares about
Buchanan, and when he picks up the toaster and clock with
which he has been presented and joins the lunch queue, '*No
one speaks to him or is aware of his presence*' (p. 161). In
Scene 16, when Buchanan returns to the firm's 'Bright
Hours' club for lonely and despairing ex-employees, the old
man who seems to recognise him has really mistaken him

for a mate of his named Georgie Hyams. Despite Mrs Vealfoy and the spiritless singing of old favourites, Buchanan is not to be taken in by the corporate entertainments: 'Nobody knows me. They've never seen me before' (p. 189). He is the Invisible Man. In the violent scene that follows, he lays out his non-functioning clock and toaster on a table, *'lifts a hammer and smashes them to pieces'* (p. 190).

Buchanan's dehumanisation is grotesquely indicated by prosthetic devices: his artificial arm, his false teeth, his hearing-aid, his glasses. He needs to be reconstructed each morning when he wakes up. His death occurs wordlessly while his wife Edith is babbling on about a co-worker who is a 'dedicated holiday maker' (p. 191), about the tickets that have just arrived for the company's annual get-together at the Bell Hotel with a name band, and about their grandson Raymond who has thoroughly reformed and who will come to the ball with his wife Debbie and her parents. In the midst of this twaddle, which represents the triumph of Mrs Vealfoy and her values, Buchanan *'closes his eyes and dies'* (p. 191). This is as close to raw pathos as Orton ever comes in any of his plays. Too close perhaps because it disrupts the comic equilibrium. There is a rage in Buchanan that is entirely uncharacteristic of Orton. The divestiture scene (5), for example, is very much in the style of Brecht (compare the investiture of the Pope in *Galileo*). Completely in pantomine, we see Buchanan returning his company uniform piece by piece. The tailor's dummy that receives the uniform is glorified, while the poor Buchanan in his street clothes *'appears smaller, shrunken and insignificant'* (p. 164). A brilliant scene, but too symbolic for comedy, too evocative of strong feeling. In *The Erpingham Camp* all feeling is scrupulously refrigerated and depersonalised.

Young Ray, Buchanan and Edith's grandson, begins the play with his own declaration of independence:

RAY: I don't work.

BUCHANAN: Not work!? (*He stares, open-mouthed.*) What do you do then?

RAY: I enjoy myself.

BUCHANAN: That's a terrible thing to do. (p. 167)

Personal enjoyment is the enemy of the corporation and the corporate state. Like Sloane, Ray recreates his culture from the flotsam and jetsam of the mass media. His 'serious talk' with his grandfather, Buchanan, has the patterned absurdity of a Mr Interlocutor and Mr Bones dialogue. Buchanan asks: 'Something's missing from your life. Do you know what it is?' Ray tentatively proposes: 'Is it God?' But Buchanan is suspicious of being put on: 'Who told you about Him?' Ray identifies his intellectual and theological sources with candour: 'I read a bit in the paper once' (p. 172).

Ironically, Ray is processed into the work ethic not by Buchanan's boring homilies, but by his affair with Debbie Fieldman and her subsequent pregnancy. In this, too, Mrs Vealfoy is the manipulating force that socialises Ray and brings him simultaneously to the altar and to the workplace. Ray's perfunctory 'Yes' touches off Mrs Vealfoy's aria of optimistic puffery: 'Ah, I'm glad you used that particular word. An affirmation of anything is cheering nowadays. Say "Yes" as often as possible, Raymond, I always do. (*Laughs.*) Always. (*Smiles.*)' (p. 181). Ray has no way to resist this sort of attack, and once he has filled out the forms Mrs Vealfoy gives him, his life as a free spirit is over. He is on his way to becoming another Buchanan.

In the year that separated *The Good and Faithful Servant* (1964) from *The Erpingham Camp* (1965), Orton had learned how to write a political play without lapsing into allegory, ideological pantomime or deeply felt personal statement. Erpingham is closely related to Mrs Vealfoy. Both are spokesmen for the establishment, for upper-middle-class business and Tory values, for law and order and the status quo, but in *The Erpingham Camp* there is a genuine popular uprising among the campers, a Peasants' Revolt, that calls these values into question. In this play both anarchy and paternalistic dictatorship are seen to be equally unattractive, so that we finish with a standoff between victims and victimisers. But the ending of the play reasserts the grandiosely imperial mission of Erpingham, as he is martyred by the angry mob: he *'abruptly disappears through a hole which opens up in the floor'* (p. 317). This strange event ends the revolution, and in the final tableau the charismatic and quasi-religious emanation of the Great Leader, like Winston Churchill in *What the Butler Saw*, is once more insisted on: *'The body of* ERPINGHAM *is left alone in the moonlight with the red balloons and dying flames in a blaze from the distant stained glass. A great choir is heard singing "The Holy City"* ' (p. 320). Orton is a master of believable Kitsch.

The point is that Erpingham is an authentic 'figure of authority' (p. 303). True to his own third-rate vision of a world conquered by entertainment, he speaks in the synthetically poetic language of glossy ads:

> Rows of Entertainment Centres down lovely, unspoiled bits of the coast, across deserted moorland and barren mountainside. The Earthly Paradise. Ah . . .
> *He stares raptly into the distance.*

I can hear it. I can touch it. And the sight of it is
hauntingly beautiful, Riley.   (p. 281)

We recognise the saccharine voice-over of travelogues.
Erpingham has an alarming tendency to speak in capital-
ised abstractions that parody both poetry and oratory: 'The
Vision that delighted has gone' (p. 282), 'Let the spirit of
Enterprise and Achievement go with you. Remember our
Glorious Dead' (p. 288), 'It's my intention to defy the
forces of Anarchy with all that is best in twentieth century
civilization' (p. 308). His Victorian propriety and fervent
monarchism are anachronistically touching: 'I am going to
undress, Padre. Cover up the portrait of Her Majesty' (p.
289). It is only when the Great Leader is fully invested in
his corset and tails that he allows the Queen's portrait to be
uncovered: 'Take the blindfold from Her Majesty. I can
give her an audience now' (p. 292).

Erpingham's seriousness and humourlessness can also be
seen as insufferable pomposity, cant and prudery. He is a
latter-day Malvolio, a 'kind of Puritan' (*Twelfth Night*
2.3.140), and a sworn enemy to pleasure. One of Erpingham's first acts in the play is to decree that a pair of plastic
ducks that have become stuck together must be summarily
dealt with: 'I want those ducks destroyed. We've no time
for hedonists here. My camp is a pure camp' (p. 279). Thus
when Erpingham confronts the Bacchic rioters, his only
defence is to insist on keeping up appearances. He is
shocked by Ted's lack of trousers: 'I don't allow indecent
exposure in my camp. Consult the manual' (p. 302). The
camp manual is a cross between the Bible and a book of
etiquette. When Erpingham reports on the frenzied chaos
he has witnessed, his language becomes more and more
elocutionary, circumlocutory and bureaucratic: 'It would
take the pen of our National poet to describe the scene that

met my eyes upon entering the Grand Ballroom' (pp. 304–5). Sexual licence is, of course, as in Euripides' *Bacchae*, the main component of the popular uprising: 'They were running about half-naked spewing up their pork'n beans. I counted eight pairs of women's briefs on the stairs. There'll be some unexpected visits to the pre-natal clinic after tonight' (p. 304). Throughout the rioting Kenny is dressed in his contestant's costume of a leopard skin, like Sergeant Match's leopard-spotted dress in *What the Butler Saw*. This animal reminiscence of the God Hercules' lion skin contrasts sharply with Erpingham's formal attire.

The conflict between Erpingham and the rioters is partly a clash of language and gesture, with all their class implications. When the pregnant Eileen hits Erpingham on the back of the head with a bottle, the Padre is 'White-faced' with shock: 'That's Mr Erpingham! ... You've struck a figure of authority!' (p. 303). Erpingham rises painfully to his full dignity and '*turns coldly upon* EILEEN': 'You are banned from the Erpingham Camp for life!' This is a parody of the expulsion from Paradise, with appropriate Miltonic echoes, but Eileen's only reaction is to make 'a farting noise,' the British equivalent of the Bronx cheer. Later, when Erpingham confronts the violent Kenny, the acknowledged lower-class leader of the uprising, he can only deal with him in the '*quiet contempt*' (p. 306) of class distinctions: 'You stand dressed in a leopard skin and woolly cardigan calling on logic? You're like an atheist praying to his God.'

With smiling disdain Erpingham coolly puts the anarchic Kenny in his place by denying the inalienable rights of man guaranteed by Paine, Rousseau, Locke and the Declaration of Independence: 'You have no rights. You have certain privileges which can be withdrawn. I am withdrawing them' (p. 307). To Erpingham's monarchic rhetoric Kenny can

only reply: 'You'll pay for this, you ignorant fucker!'
Kenny's vulgarism draws *'cries of horror from the staff'*.
The underlying irony of Erpingham's prudery and attack
on pleasure in a camp devoted to Entertainment is not lost
on the revolutionaries. Scene 10 represents the triumph of
the lower orders as they break open the Stores to the
accompaniment of 'La Marseillaise'. Both Kenny and
Eileen speak in the popular rhetoric of the French Revolution: 'Piss off you dirty middle-class prat! And take your
poxy wife with you' (p. 311), 'Have a bash, I say. Have a
bash for the pregnant woman next door!' (p. 310).

Erpingham's punctiliousness about ceremony links this
play with the bureaucratic mannerisms of Mrs Vealfoy, but
Erpingham is a more complex character. He is no faceless
functionary like Mrs Vealfoy. His role is constantly energised by a blatantly mercenary charlatanism that is missing
from the Director of Personnel, who does her job with
mindless enthusiasm. There is nothing mindless about the
grandiose Erpingham, even though he speaks in the empty
jargon of administrative authority. He has a genius for
ritualistic detail. Thus when the drunken and incompetent
stage Irishman, Chief Redcoat Riley, is endowed with the
insignia of the Chief Entertainments Officer, the ceremony
is elaborately solemn and the presence of the Padre gives it
the proper religious unction: 'ERPINGHAM *takes a box from
the desk and hands it to the* PADRE. *The* PADRE *takes a sash
from the box which he hands to* ERPINGHAM. RILEY *bows his
head.* ERPINGHAM *puts the sash upon him'* (p. 288). A badge
is then ceremoniously pinned on Riley's blazer. Suddenly,
'RILEY *is bathed in an unearthly radiance'*, and we hear the
music of 'Zadok the Priest and Nathan the Prophet
Anointed Solomon King'.

Incidentally, this is the play in which Orton uses music
most extensively to underline his ironic points. The proces-

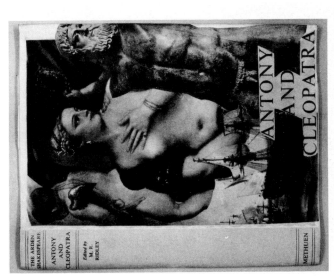

1. Orton and Halliwell's flamboyant collage for the Arden edition of *Antony and Cleopatra*, published by Methuen, and for the *Collins Guide to Roses*.

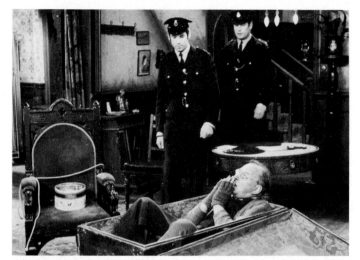

2.(a) The ex-priest McCorquodale (Bill Fraser) outfacing the police in the
Yorkshire Television production of *Funeral Games*. 1968.

2.(b) Caulfield (Ian McShane) the Private Eye, interrogating Tessa (Vivien
Merchant) in *Funeral Games*.

3. The Bacchic entertainments in *The Erpingham Camp*, with Erpingham officiating in full dress. Kings Head Theatre, London, 1979.

4. The marriage ceremony at the end of the film version of *Entertaining Mr Sloane* (1969), directed by Douglas Hickox, in which Ed (Harry Andrews) and his sister Kath (Beryl Reid) discover a beautiful solution to their sexual problems. Peter McEnery as Sloane.

5. Beryl Reid as Kath inveigling the young Sloane (Malcolm McDowell) in her grandiose plans for the future. Royal Court Theatre, London, 1975.

6. Mr McLeavy (Milo O'Shea) appears to instruct the canny Inspector Truscott (Richard Attenborough) in the film version of *Loot*, 1970. An Arthur Lewis production for British Lion.

7.   Nurse Fay settles on Dennis for her new husband. *Loot*, 1970.

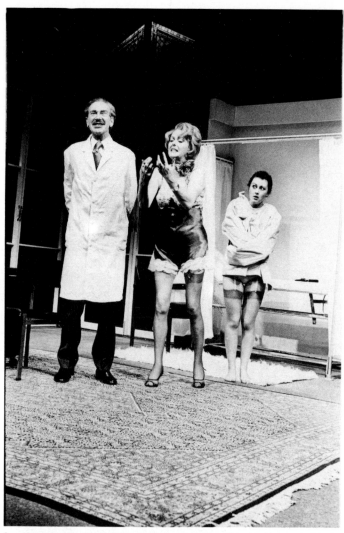

8. Mrs Prentice (Betty Marsden) expostulating with the imperturbable Dr Rance (Valentine Dyall) who has just placed Geraldine (Jane Carr) in a strait jacket in *What the Butler Saw*, Royal Court Theatre, London, 1975.

sion of cold meats on their trolley – the *'hams, cold chickens, sausages, a pig's head and trotters'* (p. 301) that the campers will never taste – is accompanied by the Dead March from *Saul*. A ceremonial disaster is in the air. Riley's operatic investiture is reversed with equal gravity in Scene 9, when Erpingham strips his honours from him to the sound of a single trumpet: 'Give me your sash and medal. You've proved yourself unworthy of them' (p. 305). Medal for what, we may well ask, but authority needs ritual to assert its prerogatives.

In addition to secular ceremony, formal religion plays an important role in *The Erpingham Camp*. The Padre is a scapegrace figure who still has the authority of a defrocked priest. 'You're interested in religion then, Padre?' asks Erpingham rather superfluously, but the Padre replies with sly wit: 'From a purely Christian point of view, sir' (p. 291). This is one among many of Orton's packaged question-and-answer gags that remind us of radio comedy or music hall dialogue. The Padre's intended sermon on the Gadarene swine (Matthew 8:28) – a story of frenzy and exorcism – also has a witty moral: 'We are meant to understand, sir, that with madness, as with vomit, it's the passer-by who receives the inconvenience' (p. 290). This anticipates the demonic madness of the camp revolt, and Erpingham, the Tory politician, is rightly disturbed: 'I don't feel that the story of the Gadarene swine has any real meaning for us today' (p. 292). Meanwhile the Padre is requested to be at the bathing beauty contest because 'A clerical face always inspires confidence at a gathering of semi-nude women' (p. 299), and in the evening he is to 'mingle with the older men and tell a few of your "off-colour" stories'.

Religion, or the illusion thereof, is crucial to a play that deals almost entirely in appearances. It is political in the sense that its public ceremony is a manifestation of authority and power. As a final, desperate gesture, Erpingham sends the Padre, with a borrowed crucifix, accompanied by the entertainer Jessie Mason, 'a simple Virgin' (p. 313) – but elsewhere identified as the 'resident nymphomaniac' (p. 295) – to pacify the angry rabble in imitation of Raphael's painting, 'Pope Leo turning back the Hordes of Attila'. The ritual effect is powerful: '*The* PADRE, *followed by* JESSIE MASON, *cross, slowly, with great dignity. A lambent light, not of this world, accompanies them*' (p. 314). The music is Gounod's 'Ave Maria'. There is a sudden silence, and the ceremonial ruse almost works, but the mob is soon trampling the man of God and his acolyte. When Erpingham hears that his Canvatex Van Gogh has been torn to shreds, he knows that the end is near: 'We'll have a couple of verses of "Love Divine, All Love Excelling", Padre. It's fire-hoses, tear-gas and the boot from then on' (p. 315). Unlike *Funeral Games*, which turns entirely on religious cant and fakery, *The Erpingham Camp* satirises religion as a representative of authority and the state. The rhetoric and ceremony of the church lend themselves to political symbolism, since Erpingham's empire is at heart a theocracy founded on entertainment.

The mutiny in the camp sweeps away all the external forms of decency and propriety – 'Twenty Christian centuries in the dust' (p. 315), as Erpingham phrases it – but the revolutionaries are as stultified and as rhetorically self-indulgent as the system they are trying to replace. We are left with cynical conclusions about the overthrow of one authority by another even more debased and mindless. In the very first scene of the play, Riley warns Erpingham about the wheel of Fortune and the Pride that goeth before a Fall, hints passed on by 'an old lay sister who'd once been an usherette at the Roxy' (p. 282). Erpingham angrily insists: 'We live in a rational world, Riley. I've no use for your Hibernian cant.' Similarly, Kenny's violence is almost the first thing we learn about him. Like Lenny in Pinter's *The Homecoming* (written in 1964), he deals with a troublesome reality in a perfectly natural way. Not knowing how to handle his stubborn and objecting in-laws, he finds a simple solution: 'In the end I bashed them both about the ear. And after that we had no trouble' (p. 284). Both Kenny's violence and Erpingham's ceremonial rationalism mirror each other. They are essentially political attitudes, a way of asserting authority over a resistant, intractable and almost meaningless reality.

5
Occulted Discourse and Threatening Nonsense in 'Entertaining Mr. Sloane'

In its root sense, the occult is that which is hidden,
concealed or covered over in order to protect arcane truths
from the eyes of the uninitiated. In other words, there is a
sharp contrast between the manifest and the latent meanings. 'Contrast' may be too mild a word because the most
likely form of relation between surface and implied meanings is one of contradiction. The stated meaning is bland,
polite, innocuous, even vacuous, in order to conceal a
violent, chaotic and painful truth. To formulate this double
effect in a different way, we may say that the language is
deliberately and systematically occulted in order to sustain
a continuous irony between what is said and what is meant.
In popular parlance, language as an expressive vehicle is
rendered meaningless, banal and jejune so that the real
tenor and purpose of that language may be safely pro-

tected. Harsh truths are insulated by the trite formulae of social discourse. The characters speak an amusing and titilating babble of stock phrases, trite moralising (often of a proverbial turn), and pre-packaged emotional clichés drawn from the stockpot of daytime television serials. When this style is cultivated self-consciously by the author, the effect is that of collage, because the author is aiming at an occult contrast between the nonsense that is revealed and the deeper meanings that lie hidden. In this limited sense, the author is using a secret language for his surface discourse.

We are speaking of a general tendency in contemporary literature to appropriate non-literary materials and to employ them in disguised and ironic ways. No modern playwright uses this occulted discourse (or threatening nonsense) more brilliantly than Joe Orton. It is completely natural for a working-class lad from Leicester, a homosexual without any gifts or talents that anyone had ever noticed, to disguise his rage and disappointment with life in a jokester's or trickster's blank discourse. There is no way to deal directly with the monolithic society from which one has been forcibly excluded. As the self-appointed 'fly on the wall' (Lahr, p. 28), Orton's buzzing was not overtly aggressive or harmful; it was merely intended to disturb the complacency of its targets. The image is emphatically a fly and not a wasp or mosquito.

It is in this area that one may understand how superficial Orton's relation is to Pinter, the model for his early plays. Orton ruthlessly cuts away Pinter's 'significances', so that comedy of menace would seem a pretentious and misguided term for Orton's savage, anarchic and turbulent farces of daily life and its empty deceptions. His sense of language as farcical exhibitionism undercuts and neutralises any feeling of menace. Orton does not write comedies of menace, but rather comedies of need and greed, where the only truths behind a façade of epigrammatic and pointless discourse are those generated by the blind instincts of self-preservation and self-aggrandisement. In this sense, unthinking egoism and self-expression are the only realities in Orton's world.

Entertaining Mr. Sloane (1963) is so distressingly auto-biographical that it offers the most explicit illustrations of Orton's occulted discourse. We know from Lahr's biography that the old and more or less useless Dadda, Kemp, is modelled on Orton's own father, that the sentimentally lascivious housewife Kath draws largely on Orton's mother, and that the idle, violent and bisexual drifter, Sloane, has many qualities of the playwright himself. The play is suffused with a sense of grandiloquence, a height-ened style that is the language of a preposterous self-love. In other words, the style is continuously inflated as the tired platitudes of middle-class respectability are trolled out to decorate the naked lust, greed and aggression of the characters. The thin and shabby veneer of civilisation very imperfectly hides the monstrous truths on which the action is based.

The central event of the play is that Sloane brutally kills Ed's and Kath's old father, who happens to know about an earlier murder that Sloane had committed. The homosexual brother, Ed, and the whorish-motherly Kath both desperately need Sloane as confidant and lover, so that Sloane's murder of their father has absolutely no moral resonance. There is no real question of turning Sloane over to the police – only a question of Ed's and Kath's bargaining with each other to 'find a basis for agreement' (p. 134). The negotiations are conducted under a barrage of meaningless assertions about law, order and decency. As a street-wise kid, Sloane knows that Ed and Kath are only spouting worn-out formulae that have no relevance to the present situation. Their mechanical moralising will cosset and flatter their own respectable consciences while Sloane can choose the best deal that will keep him out of prison and provide for his material comfort. He can rely on Ed's and Kath's rampant sexuality to protect him. The language of the play is only a bubble and froth of words meant to embellish the harsh, implicit truths that cannot be spoken. It all sounds like a parody of the empty slogans of welfare state paternalism, and the painfully moralistic phrases are no more than babble. As Orton wrote in his diary, 'The whole trouble with Western society today is the lack of anything worth concealing' (Lahr, p. 131).

Although Orton's work was undoubtedly shaped by early Pinter, *Entertaining Mr. Sloane*, written a year before Pinter's *The Homecoming* (1964), seems to have influenced that play. Pinter's Ruth develops the mother-whore stereotype of Orton's Kath and, more pointedly, Pinter's overbearing hustler, Lenny, has a type resemblance to Orton's hollowly successful and vaguely criminal Ed. Both are full of insufferable pretensions to middle-class manners and style. Both Lenny and Ed speak a language that is peculiarly synthetic and literary – a language of disguise that is entirely stripped of any affect, emotion or human resonance. Thus, when Ed learns that his sister is having sexual relations with Sloane and is, in fact, pregnant, he reacts with a cool and vituperative eloquence:

What a little whoreson you are you little whoreson. You are a little whoreson and no mistake. I'm put out my boy. Choked. (*Pause*.) What attracted you? Did she give trading stamps? You're like all these layabouts. Kiddies with no fixed abode. (p. 119)

The stilted diction, including the archaic 'whoreson', and the posed emotions – 'Choked' – contain the violence. It is all very stagey and histrionic, but threatening nevertheless. Ed is speaking for his own pleasure rather than from any need to communicate with Mr Sloane. The message is fixed for Sloane by Ed's icy detachment.

The formulaic quality of the speech in *Entertaining Mr. Sloane* emphasises the isolation of the characters from each other. Everyone seems to be talking to himself or herself, except perhaps for the old father, Kemp, who has a dangerous secret to tell about Sloane's past and who winds up dead for his troubles. Orton seems to deny any possibility of communication, so that language is almost by definition occult, because it serves chiefly as a way of concealing meaning. Once this assumption is accepted, it becomes easier to feel the strength of Orton's sardonic playfulness. For the staging of *What the Butler Saw*, we know that Orton typed up a list of phrases that could be used *ad libitum* by the cast for comic putdowns: 'You revolting fur-covered bitch!'; 'You shoulder-length prick!'; 'He likes women – you know, strip clubs, menstruation, mothers-in-law'; and the Wildean epigram: 'A word not in current use except in the vernacular' (Lahr, p. 258). Orton could afford to be in love with language for its own sake, because the words are so separated from any determinative meaning.

Some of Sloane's speeches are detachable arias, little pop culture vignettes of hard-boiled sentimentality, such as his extravagant narration to Kemp of the circumstances leading to his first murder:

It's like this see. One day I leave the Home. Stroll along. Sky blue. Fresh air. They'd found me a likeable permanent situation. Canteen facilities. Fortnight's paid holi-

day. Overtime? Time and a half after midnight. A staff
dance each year. What more could one wish to devote
one's life to? I certainly loved that place. The air round
Twickenham was like wine. Then one day I take a trip to
the old man's grave. Hic Jacets in profusion. Ashes to
Ashes. Alas the fleeting. The sun was declining. A few
press-ups on a tomb belonging to a family name of
Cavaneagh, and I left the graveyard.   (pp. 124–5)

This is fashioned in the mock-pastoral, mock-poetic mode,
with air 'like wine', bits and pieces of tombstone inscrip-
tions, and a part-line from 'The Rose of Tralee' ('The sun
was declining'). Sloane is exuberant as he leads up to his
encounter with the erotic photographer who liked 'certain
interesting features I had that he wanted the exclusive right
of preserving' (p. 125). The blatant sexuality is always
guarded and disguised – not part of a system of pleasure or
hedonism, but only an expression of need and greed, the
overpowering desire to use and possess another person.

Sloane's style collects fragments and puts them together
in a pattern that has no relation at all to any meaningful
context of ordinary discourse. The fragments are displaced
and juxtaposed so that they have what Orton called a
'collage quality' (Lahr, p. 154). His room with Halliwell
was an enormous collage of pasted-up images, and they
both were sent to prison in 1962 for their extraordinary
collage effects in public library books, especially on the
altered dust jackets. In the bewildering welter of media
inputs and pop culture imagery, Orton took seriously his
role as collagist:

Shakespeare and the Elizabethans did the same thing. I
mean you have absolute realism and then you get high
poetry, it's just language. I think you should use the

language of your age and every bit of it. They always go on about poetic drama and they think you have to sort of go off in some high-flown fantasy, but it isn't poetic, it's everything, it's the language in use at the time.

(Lahr, p. 154)

But Sloane's eloquence and Orton's eloquence are extremely self-conscious. The comparison with Shakespeare and the Elizabethans is apt because Orton wrote with such bravado. In its exuberance and flamboyance, his style is certainly closer to Marlowe's than to Shakespeare's, but perhaps closest of all to the mysterious Cyril Tourneur of *The Revenger's Tragedy* (*c.* 1607).[1]

Orton delights in collecting sentimental clichés for the part of Kath, the fading, mock-voluptuous mother-whore, who seduces Sloane and mothers him without any feeling of contradiction. Kath is the consumerist *par excellence* of the ladies' magazines, and she lives in a world of tawdry, commercialised romance. Her knick-knacks define both her respectability and her illusions about the existence of a larger world outside her own house, which is pointedly located in the middle of a garbage dump. Her 'sophisticated' conversation with Sloane is all mindless twaddle, civilised foreplay leading up to the sex act:

KATH: Isn't this room gorgeous?

SLOANE: Yes.

KATH: That vase over there comes from Bombay. Do you have any interest in that part of the world?

SLOANE: I like Dieppe.

KATH: Ah . . . it's all the same. I don't suppose they know the difference themselves.

(p. 93)

Kath's Bombay and Sloane's Dieppe are both cities of the

mind, high-sounding words for places that have no reality. Kath's discourse has no relation to her transparent negligee, with which she is teasing Sloane: 'I blame it on the manufacturers. They make garments so thin nowadays you'd think they intend to provoke a rape' (p. 93). By the time she is rolling on top of Sloane, he has become her baby: 'What a big heavy baby you are. Such a big heavy baby' (p. 95). Kath dresses up her naked need for Sloane's body in a variety of genteel clichés, but the language moves on an entirely separate plane from the realities of seduction. When Sloane threatens to leave the pregnant Kath after the murder of Kemp she trolls out all the warmed-over tag lines of soap opera: 'I've a bun in the oven', 'Mr. Sloane was nice to me', 'He's free with me', 'Can't manage without a woman' (pp. 139, 141). Kath is the archetype of all injured women, both long-suffering and unappreciated mother and jilted torch-lady who has no regrets. She speaks in the parodic formulae of domestic tragedy. 'Who tucks him up at night? And he likes my cooking. He won't deny that' (p. 140). 'I gave him three meals a day. Porridge for breakfast. Meat and two veg for dinner. A fry for tea. And cheese for supper. What more could he want?' (p. 141). A lascivious Mrs Portnoy, who has managed to preserve the integrity of English family life. What more could anyone possibly want? We know that Orton had ambiguous feelings about his cold, sexless, very respectable, but nevertheless seductive mother. Kath projects a powerful incest fantasy of the omnipotent mother who is sexual and nurturing at the same time, but whose overwhelming love must ultimately be rejected by her guilty, adolescent son. According to Freud's formulation in 'The Most Prevalent Form of Degradation in Erotic Life' (1912), the fear of incest in the mother-whore situation often produces male impotence.

Orton dramatises his own sexual ambiguity in the struggle between Kath and Ed for the control of Sloane's body. The play has a surprising bisexual conclusion, but the language throughout is intensely misogynistic. Ed has a whole series of apothegms for putting women in their place: 'Women are like banks, boy, breaking and entering is a serious business. Give me your word you're not vaginalatrous?' (p. 88). 'Vaginalatrous' is an Orton coinage on analogy with 'idolatrous'; it indicates a perverse attachment. To Ed, women are essentially frivolous vamps intent on deceiving men: 'The way these birds treat decent fellows. I hope you never get serious with one. What a life. Backache, headache or her mum told her never to when there's an "R" in the month' (p. 113). This is an old formula, on analogy with the popular prohibition against eating oysters except in months with an 'R', that seems to turn on disgust at menstruation. When Ed is grappling with Kath for Sloane in the last act, he is not above insulting her physically, as if she were the archetypal woman: 'Flabby mouth. Wrinkled neck. Puffy hands.' 'Sagging tits.' 'Sawdust up to the navel' (pp. 142–3). Her genitalia are scored off in a parody of Dante: 'You showed him the gate of Hell every night. He abandoned Hope when he entered there' (p. 143). As a sexual being, Kath can only be shown histrionically. In an exaggerated gesture, she offers Sloane her hand: 'Kiss my hand, dear, in the manner of the theatre', and Ed's final insult is to Kath as an actress, falsely evoking theatrical sentiment: 'What a cruel performance you're giving. Like an old tart grinding to her climax' (p. 143). The old tart, of course, mocks both sexuality and the theatre. Ed's language of vituperation seems the most expressive idiom in the play, but he himself assumes a position of moral and social superiority to Kath that is based only on vigorous but hollow assertion. No moral positions are possible in this play. Everyone is wholly occupied by the narcissistic struggle for survival.

Entertaining Mr. Sloane is hardly occult in any of the popular meanings of that term, yet there is a pervasive irony by which the surface action of the play is radically different from what is really happening. On the one side we see a parody of middle-class English values, full of vain moralising and empty social gestures. On the other are power and greed nakedly striving to fulfil themselves without regard to human values. Behind the comedy of manners façade, aggressive lust dominates the play. The nonsense in this play is still very threatening; it has not been neutralised by farce. We still feel the tremendous effort at concealment by which the deeper meanings have been occulted and trivialised, so that turbulence and chaos are only imperfectly mastered. It is gradually becoming apparent that Orton belongs in the classic tradition of English comedy that includes Swift, Wycherley and Wilde. In his own disguised and farcical way, Orton sought to make contact with bitter truths. Beneath the occulted and at times nonsensical collage of pop culture dialogue, Orton tried for an emotional effect like Swift's savage indignation.

6
'Loot' as Quotidian Farce: The Intersection of Black Comedy and Daily Life

After his mother died, one of the few remembrances Joe Orton wanted to preserve was his mother's teeth. In his sardonic private mythology of realism, he insisted that the cast of *Loot* confront this totemic object. It was a symbolic gesture to prevent the play from lapsing into an empty and mechanical farce. The style of *Loot* raised special difficulties for both the director and the actors that provoked endless rewrites. These problems brought the cast to the very edge of hysteria.

Loot *as Quotidian Farce*

The dentures of the dead Mrs McLeavy figure impor-
tantly in a bizarre scene in Act One of *Loot* where Nurse
Fay is undressing the corpse and has already handed across
the screen, '*in quick succession, a pair of corsets, a brassiere
and a pair of knickers*' (p. 227). She asks: 'Are you
committed to having her teeth removed?', and Hal, the
homosexual, bank-robbing son answers, 'Yes'. Meanwhile,
Hal is fantasising about the two-star or three-star brothel
he will run with the loot from the bank robbery:

> I'd advertise 'By Appointment'. Like jam . . . I'd have
> a French bird, a Dutch bird, a Belgian bird, an Italian
> bird –
> FAY *hands a pair of false teeth across the screen.*
> – and a bird that spoke fluent Spanish and performed
> the dance of her native country to perfection. (*He
> clicks the teeth like castanets.*) I'd call it the Consum-
> matum Est. And it'd be the most famous house of
> ill-fame in the whole of England.
> FAY *appears from behind the screen.* HAL *holds up the
> teeth.* These are good teeth. Are they the National
> Health?
> FAY. No. She bought them out of her winnings. She had
> some good evenings at the table last year.
>
> (pp. 226–7)

We can readily understand why Kenneth Cranham
looked very sick and Simon Ward shook like jelly when
Orton handed around his mother's teeth 'like nuts at
Christmas' (p. 272); as the hard-boiled detective Truscott
says: 'Your sense of detachment is terrifying, lad. Most
people would at least flinch upon seeing their mother's eyes

and teeth handed around like nuts at Christmas' (p. 272). Orton was cutting through the artificialities and the stilted conventions of West End farce to make a point about what we might call 'quotidian farce', which is much closer to black comedy than to the upper-class, comedy-of-manners assumptions of Restoration comedy, or even the middle-class gentility that Feydeau so deftly titillated in his brilliant social comedies. Orton is returning farce to its roots in Plautus and the Italic fertility and harvest rituals that farce celebrates. Like Plautus, Orton is crude and vulgar, although in Orton the language and the action seem to be moving in entirely opposite directions. Thus Hal speaks with affected chic (and a learned pun) of his new brothel, the Consummatum Est, while clicking his mother's false teeth like castanets. Death as the ultimate tabooed subject (with sex a close second) is also the optimum subject to energise a vulgar, realistic farce cloaked in the empty, genteel clichés of the English Welfare State.

Apparently Orton's mother, Elsie, was very fastidious about her dentures, which she kept soaking in bleach in order to produce a blindingly white, million dollar smile. As Kath, the mother-whore of *Entertaining Mr. Sloane*, says in her apology to the young lodger/sex object Sloane:

> My teeth, since you mentioned the subject, Mr Sloane, are in the kitchen in Stergene. Usually I allow a good soak overnight. But what with one thing and another I forgot. Otherwise I would never be in such a state. (*Pause.*) I hate people who are careless with their dentures. (p. 90)

Everywhere in Orton's life and work he is mocking insufferable pretensions to middle-class propriety. This is quotidian farce in its most literal sense, since the plays feed on the endless preoccupations of daily life. The lewd, possessive Kath, moving through the play by amoral animal instinct, spends most of her aimless day keeping up appearances. Thus in the beautifully ironic curtain line of *Loot*, the nurse/murderer Fay insists sharply that once she is married to Dennis they will have to move out of Hal's house. 'People would talk. We must keep up appearances.' And the play ends with a sanctimonious tableau: '*She returns to her prayers, her lips move silently.* DENNIS *and* HAL *at either side of the coffin*' (p. 275).

Loot is still highly autobiographical, but less consistently so than *Entertaining Mr. Sloane* of a year earlier. Like Synge, Orton was constantly copying phrases and anecdotes of street life into his abundant notebooks. And he thought of himself as radically different from Pinter. He wanted his first Pinteresque play, *The Ruffian on the Stair*, to be as unlike Pinter as possible:

> The play is clearly not written naturalistically, but it must be directed and acted with absolute *realism*. No 'stylization', no 'camp'. . . . Everything the characters say is *true*. . . . The play mustn't be presented as an example of the now out-dated 'mystery' school – *vide* early Pinter. Everything is as clear as the most reactionary *Telegraph* reader could wish. There is a beginning, a middle and an end. . . . (Lahr, p. 130)

Orton was preoccupied with the 'realism' of dentures and dialogue because traditional farce was so highly stylised. The realism would contribute to the abrasive juxtaposition of black comedy and daily life. The point, of course, is that black comedy by its very nature as comedy is abstracted from daily life and insulated from any sense of pain and injury. Orton's quotidian farce is a contradiction in terms, or at least a paradox of the comic imagination, since farce is traditionally an unreal, highly mannered, dreamlike management of our naked aggressions.[1] Orton enjoyed working against the grain.

Quotidian farce has its roots in pop culture. We are not surprised to find Dennis, the luxurious undertaker's assistant, putting a piece of chewing gum in his mouth at a critical moment (p. 206), then later sticking it *'under the coffin'* (p. 210). Hal says that he got the idea of hiding the money in a coffin from 'the comics I read' (p. 207). Wherever we turn in *Loot*, we are assaulted by the vulgar bits and pieces of daily life, usually fantasticated by Orton's impudent imagination. Hal, for example, wants to celebrate his success by taking Dennis to 'a remarkable brothel I've found. Really remarkable. Run by three Pakistanis aged between ten and fifteen. They do it for sweets. Part of their religion. Meet me at seven. Stock up with Mars bars' (p. 267). It is curious that among the pseudonymous letters Orton wrote under the outraged housewife persona of Mrs Edna Welthorpe is one dated 14 April 1967, attacking *Loot* for the second act discussion 'upon the raping of children with Mars bars . . .' (Lahr, p. 227). These, and 'other filthy details of a sexual and psychopathic nature . . .,' do not, of course, appear in *Loot*, but Orton took particular delight in outraging the insatiable popular longing for and loathing of pornography.

Loot has an abundance of homosexual 'in' jokes. Dennis, for example, refuses to go to a brothel with Hal: 'I'm on the wagon. I'm trying to get up sufficient head of steam to marry' (p. 209). Dennis would like to get married because 'it's the one thing I haven't tried', but Hal upbraids him: 'I don't like your living for kicks, baby. Put these neurotic ideas out of your mind and concentrate on the problems of

everyday life' (p. 210). When Fay insists that Dennis is
'more relaxed in the company of women', Truscott takes
this as gay innuendo: 'He'll have to come to terms with his
psychological peculiarity' (p. 243). These are admittedly
easy reversals, but they depend on a pop culture awareness
of sexual clichés.

Like Wilde in *The Importance of Being Earnest*, Orton as
homosexual playwright assumes the stance of alien, out-
sider, critic and satirist of *all* the values that straight
middle-class society most cherishes. There is a cheerful
anarchy about Orton's works, in which nothing can be
assumed, and in which all values – including the shibboleths
of sexuality – are up for grabs. This endows his plays with a
'carnivalesque' quality (in Bakhtin's terms), so that if he
works with the quotidian materials of pop culture and daily
life, these resources are transformed by the powers of farce.
Orton quickly learned how to use grotesquely realistic
materials without apology and without explanation. Thus
all ideology in Orton becomes a collection of meaningless
formulae. When McLeavy, the only honest, solid citizen of
Loot, protests against his false arrest, he uses the cant
phrases of democratic, civil liberties sermonising: 'You can't
do this. I've always been a law-abiding citizen' (p. 274).
This is the mediamessage, doublespeak, psychobabble that
has nothing whatsoever to do with life as it is actually lived.
In Fay's terms, McLeavy is 'such an innocent', 'Not familiar
with the ways of the world' (p. 204); to Truscott his
credulousness makes him 'a thoroughly irresponsible individual' (p. 262).

Loot is drenched in popular clichés and stereotyped
banalities. No one is more polite or thoughtful or sensitive
to the needs of others than Nurse Fay, the patient killer,
who has 'practised her own form of genocide for a decade
and called it nursing' (p. 254). In a reversal of the

Bluebeard legend, she now has her sights set for McLeavy, the bereaved widower. As the play opens, she has brought McLeavy a flower:

> MCLEAVY: That's a nice thought. (*Taking the flower from her.*)
> FAY: I'm a nice person. One in a million. (p. 195)

'Nice' is a polite formula that covers so many possible meanings and social implications that it is virtually meaningless.

Orton chooses to begin his play with the mechanised dialogue of daytime serials and soap operas in order to conceal the viciousness that lurks just below the surface. Is Fay really 'a nice person', 'One in a million'? To all intents and purposes she is a devoted and devout Catholic woman of twenty-eight, but the next bit of mindless dialogue already begins to plant seeds of doubt in our minds:

> MCLEAVY: Are those Mrs McLeavy's slippers?
> FAY: Yes. She wouldn't mind my having them.
> MCLEAVY: Is the fur genuine?
> FAY: It's fluff, not fur.
> MCLEAVY: It looks like fur.
> FAY: (*standing to her feet*). No. It's a form of fluff. They manufacture it in Leeds. (p. 195)

Fluff or fur? Why Leeds and not Leicester (where Orton was born)? Does it really matter? But why is the nurse already wearing the dead woman's slippers? Our suspicions run in the familiar channels of Grade B movies, in which fluff has an entirely different symbolic value from genuine fur.

Fay's assertions of innocence are just as sloganistic as

those of McLeavy; they are the empty phrases of an egalitarian society, which do not impress the very practical Truscott:

FAY: You must prove me guilty. That is the law.
TRUSCOTT: You know nothing of the law. I know nothing of the law. That makes us equal in the sight of the law.
FAY: I'm innocent till I'm proved guilty. This is a free country. The law is impartial.
TRUSCOTT: Who's been filling your head with that rubbish? (p. 254)

The dialogue is Gilbert-and-Sullivan musical comedy; it has no conceivable relation to beliefs or ethics. When Fay finally confesses, Truscott admires her judiciousness and professionalism: 'Very good. Your style is simple and direct. It's a theme which less skilfully handled could've given offence. . . . One of the most accomplished confessions I've heard in some time' (p. 255). In *Loot* we are constantly shifting from meaning to style, from content to form, and the whole play is delightfully self-conscious about its own means of expression. The actors are always performers, and we are never permitted to get caught up in the action. We are always aware that the epigrammatic dialogue is a script.

The lines of *Loot* are often gags from old-fashioned radio comedy, as the characters make witty repartee that has nothing to do with their characterisation; the play is divided into jokers and straight men without regard to other character functions. Thus Truscott, while questioning Hal about his mate Dennis, wants to know about the five pregnancies Dennis has on his police record:

Where does he engender these unwanted children?

Joe Orton

There are no open spaces. The police patrol regularly. It should be next to impossible to commit the smallest act of indecency, let alone beget a child. Where does he do it?

Hal answers with unexpected extravagance: 'On crowded dance floors during the rhumba' (p. 230). This is zany but it also puts down the officious Inspector Truscott; it is among many sendups in Orton of the received traditions of heterosexuality. Dennis is represented as 'A very luxurious type of lad' (p. 200), on whom 'every luxury was lavished': 'atheism, breast-feeding, circumcision' (p. 209) – again a swipe at the appurtenances of middle-class respectability. Everyone in the play speaks in one-liners and put-downs, so that the dialogue has a strongly exhibitionistic flavour. Everyone is always performing and on display.

Loot relies on the popular format of the detective story or whodunnit, although it is basically a parody of that genre – Truscott is a mock-Sherlock Holmes detective. Tom Stoppard was to parody the same genre a few years later in *The Real Inspector Hound* (1968). Proud of his accomplishments, Inspector Truscott of Scotland Yard emerges from his disguise as an official of the Water Board and formally introduces himself to McLeavy:

You have before you a man who is quite a personage in his way – Truscott of the Yard. Have you never heard of Truscott? The man who tracked down the limbless girl killer? Or was that sensation before your time?

Hal plays straight man for Truscott's gag:

HAL: Who would kill a limbless girl?
TRUSCOTT: She was the killer. (p. 250)

Like the psychiatrist Rance in *What the Butler Saw* and the bombastic camp director Erpingham in *The Erpingham Camp*, Truscott is a burlesque figure of authority who, like Jarry's Père Ubu, is grotesquely menacing. These capricious and tyrannical authority figures seemed to fascinate Orton; they appear in virtually every play he wrote.

Truscott's superlogical methods of detection are an obvious take-off on Sherlock Holmes. In the case of Nurse Fay, he knows immediately that she has a crucifix with a dent on one side that is engraved on the back: 'St Mary's Convent. Gentiles Only' (p. 214). The process of detection comes almost directly from the pages of Conan Doyle:

> My methods of deduction can be learned by anyone with a keen eye and a quick brain. When I shook your hand I felt a roughness on one of your wedding rings. A roughness I associate with powder burns and salt. The two together spell a gun and sea air. When found on a wedding ring only one solution is possible. (p. 214)

Namely, that her first husband damaged it, after which she shot him at the Hermitage Private Hotel. As Truscott explains later, 'The process by which the police arrive at the solution to a mystery is, in itself, a mystery' (pp. 250–1).

We see the Inspector in action when he comes upon Mrs McLeavy's glass eye at the end of Act One:

> *He puts his pipe into the corner of his mouth and picks up the glass eye. He holds it to the light in order to get a better view. Puzzled. He sniffs at it. He holds it close to his ear. He rattles it. He takes out a pocket magnifying-glass and stares hard at it. He gives a brief exclamation of horror and surprise.* (p. 246)

Orton is poking fun at the detective story as a genre, since it takes Truscott such an awfully long time to arrive at the horror and surprise with which any ordinary mortal would have immediately greeted the discovery of the glass eye.

Truscott is an amoral entertainer like all of Orton's authority figures, who are exceedingly articulate, assertive and self-important. He also shares with them a penchant for violence that has its roots in the gangster movies that Orton and Pinter saw in their youth. As Orton understands the Pinter influence, 'I think there are other influences on my work far more important than Pinter, and of course you always have to remember that the things which influenced Pinter, which I believe are Hollywood movies in the forties, also influenced me' (Lahr, p. 130). The gangster figure derives his power not only from the gun but also from his commanding rhetoric. Thus Truscott teases Hal with sadistic glee, as in the following dialogue:

> TRUSCOTT: (*shouting, knocking* HAL *to the floor*). Under any other political system I'd have you on the floor in tears!
> HAL: (*crying*). You've got me on the floor in tears.
>
> (p. 235)

A few lines further 'TRUSCOTT *jerks* HAL *from the floor, beating and kicking and punching him*'. Hal's screams only encourage Truscott's manic violence:

> I'll hose you down! I'll chlorinate you!
> HAL *tries to defend himself, his nose is bleeding.*
> You'll be laughing on the other side of your bloody face.
>
> (p. 236)

This kind of scene gives a special edge to Orton's quotidian

farce, since the physical cruelty denies one of the premises
of traditional farce: that the blows do not hurt and that the
characters are, by convention, insulated from pain and
punishment.

The physical violence in *Loot* drives a wedge between
the extravagant language and the more prosaic action. It
has its own special ironies because it is necessary to
preserve appearances at all costs, and especially by verbal
artifice, no matter what is actually going on. Thus Kath in
Entertaining Mr. Sloane cloaks her seduction of Sloane in
the comforting platitudes of domestic solicitude, while
Truscott insists that everyone observe the proprieties of the
English code of manners. He insists strenuously on keeping
up appearances, at least verbally, as in the scene at the end
of Act I where he cautions Dennis:

> You want to watch yourself. Making unfounded allega-
> tions. You'll find yourself in serious trouble.
> *He takes* DENNIS *by the collar and shakes him.*
> If I ever hear you accuse the police of using violence on a
> prisoner in custody again, I'll take you down to the
> station and beat the eyes out of your head.   (p. 246)

Although Truscott is a clown and a trickster, there is no
doubt at all that these are not idle threats.

As small-time hoodlums, both Dennis and Hal have a
certain warm feeling for the Inspector, who represents to
them a high level of professional accomplishment. Thus,
early in the play, Dennis acknowledges being questioned
by Truscott, who gave him 'A rabbit-type punch': 'Winded
me. Took me by the cobblers. Oh, 'strewth, it made me bad'
(p. 210). The mild oath, ' 'strewth' ('By his truth'), is a
wonderfully mannered survival of middle-class affecta-
tions, and Hal and Dennis would be virtually silent if we

discounted their high-toned euphemisms. They both speak an artificial and highly artful language that thoroughly disguises what they mean. Truscott's sadistic style is the subject of Hal's mock-admiration, as he reacts to Dennis's report of the rabbit-type punch – not, mind you, a real rabbit punch – 'Yes, he has a nice line in corporal punishment. Last time he was here he kicked my old lady's cat and he smiled while he did it' (p. 210). Corporal punishment is made respectable by being well administered. Like a salesman showing his samples, Truscott has a 'nice line' in corporal punishment, of which the ability to kick smilingly the late Mrs McLeavy's cat and the rabbit-type punch to Dennis are two convincing demonstrations.

Truscott is full of mock-indignation at the violation of proprieties. When Hal acknowledges that he would have buried the loot in holy ground, Truscott pretends to be scandalised:

> Every one of these fivers bears a portrait of the Queen. It's dreadful to contemplate the issues raised. Twenty thousand tiaras and twenty thousand smiles buried alive! She's a constitutional monarch, you know. She can't answer back.   (p. 270)

The picture of the tiaraed, smiling queen on the five pound note is invoked as an alternative to the sewing-dummy corpse of the late Mrs McLeavy and the satirical issue of *lèse-majesté* is propounded with patriotic fervour. Truscott's monarchical squeamishness is like Erpingham's insistence that the portrait of Her Majesty be covered while he dresses (p. 289).

We know, of course, that Truscott is a jester and entertainer, the comic Vice of the morality plays, but everything in *Loot* anticipates the conclusion, in which Hal, Dennis, Fay and Truscott seal their alliance with the stolen bank notes and a legalistic oblivion about poor Mrs McLeavy's murder. There are ultimately no hard feelings between the criminals and the law, who understand each other perfectly. The only victim is the priggish, smug and complacent Mr McLeavy, the only innocent in the play, who is already considered a corpse by the final tableau. It is on the fate of McLeavy that *Loot* turns sardonic. He suffers for his foolish faith in authority, but even more for his own exaggerated confidence in himself and the empty shibboleths of law and order and a rational society. When he first hears of the bank robbery, he churns out the sort of moralistic and religious twaddle that can only be offensive to the other characters; the criminals will

> have it on their conscience. Even if they aren't caught, they'll suffer. . . . Such people never benefit from their crimes. It's people like myself who have the easy time. Asleep at nights. Despite appearances to the contrary, criminals are poor sleepers. (p. 205)

Proverbially, however, the bad sleep well, and one of the morals of *Loot* is that crime pays handsomely and criminals are uniformly wittier and more charming than law-abiding citizens.

McLeavy is an insufferable apologist for the status quo, a man totally lacking in imagination and generosity. His ironic fate is set up almost from the beginning of the play, as we see him violate human values for the sake of the abstract slogans of Welfare State benevolence. When the father intones his pious and hypocritical platitudes about the police – 'I'd like to see them given wider powers. They're hamstrung by red tape. They're a fine body of men. Doing their job under impossible conditions' – his son can only cut him off with a little common sense: 'The police are a lot of idle buffoons, Dad. As you well know' (p. 206). McLeavy, of course, is the archetypal law-abiding citizen who is really a fascist at heart. Before he is caught up in the trammels of the law, he is exceedingly co-operative and wants to be of maximum assistance to authority: 'We must give this man [Truscott] every opportunity to do his duty. As a good citizen I ignore the stories which bring officialdom into disrepute' (p. 217).

We are not surprised, therefore, when the self-satisfied McLeavy refuses Truscott's reasonable offer to share in the loot:

> Now then, sir, be reasonable. . . . It's not expedient for the general public to have its confidence in the police force undermined. You'd be doing the community a grave disservice by revealing the full frightening facts of this case. (p. 271)

But McLeavy is not a 'reasonable' man nor does he understand expediency, and he is ceremoniously arrested with the words of the notorious Detective Sergeant Harold Challenor, who was much in the news at the time *Loot* was written for his excessive zeal in making arrests: 'You're fucking nicked, my old beauty' (Lahr, p. 273).[2] Orton must also have been thinking of his own spectacular arrest with Halliwell for defacing books in the Islington libraries.

Orton's plays show us a stultification of society, in which, as Simon Shepherd observes, 'people talk in received phrases, which contain their own received values, often despite what the individual really means or wants to say'. 'Everybody seems to speak journalese, to use second-hand phrases. The spoken language is so arranged that as we listen to it we hear a written text. . . . We are in the presence of the public language of Britain. Characters speak not as individuals, but as citizens, their morals are not their own but the ones they are supposed to have, they respect what they ought to respect'. Without using the phrase, Simon Shepherd gets to the heart of what I have been calling quotidian farce.

But this public language is consistently mocked in *Loot*. It is the background against which the wit, originality and initiative of the criminals are applauded, with the mad police inspector Truscott as their natural leader, while the pitifully and platitudinously law-abiding citizen, McLeavy, suffers a well-deserved martyrdom. This is as it should be in farce, where wish-fulfilment values replace the tedious assumptions of the official, patriotic pieties. The quotidian rut of daily life is exploded by the wild imagination of something else, like the sudden intrusion into the dialogue of those three Pakistani girls aged between ten and fifteen who do it for sweets – part of their religion.

To return to our original example of the dentures of Orton's deceased mother clicking like castanets in *Loot*, we may ask again in what way Orton wanted the events of the play to be thought of 'in terms of reality'? John Russell Taylor is surely wrong when he calls *Loot* 'a little arid, a play about plays and play conventions rather than a play which is, however remotely, about (if you will pardon the word) life' (p. 132). Albert Hunt rightly takes Taylor to task for failing to perceive that, despite all of its farcical and surrealistic merrymaking, *Loot* has a high degree of social consciousness. Orton points up, with some degree of bitterness and pain, the absurdities that we take for granted in our real world.

Orton was fond of the terms 'reality' and 'realistic' as a way of explaining how to stage his plays. He must surely be using these ambiguous words in the traditional sense of Synge's preface to *The Playboy of the Western World*:

> . . . in countries where the imagination of the people, and the language they use, is rich and living, it is possible for a writer to be rich and copious in his words, and at the same time to give the reality, which is the root of all poetry, in a comprehensive and natural form.

Drawing on very different sources from Synge, Orton nevertheless affirms his characters' reality by the lively, histrionic and extravagant style in which they express themselves. If the public reality is stultified, in Shepherd's sense, and the public language of Britain is torpid and dehumanising, there is an inner reality where farce inter- sects with black comedy and the characters can assert, even as a form of protest, that they are still alive. We must recognise that Orton is a social satirist like the early Shaw, and that *Loot* is a play that attacks, in the words of Albert Hunt, 'the criminal lunacy of social institutions that are generally accepted as reasonable and beneficial'.[3]

7
What Did the Butler See in 'What the Butler Saw'?

What the Butler Saw (written in 1967 and produced posthumously in 1969) is, of course, a farce without a butler, which should more properly have been called *What the Butler Might Have Seen* had there been a butler and had he been privileged to oversee the strange goings-on in Dr Prentice's private clinic. We need the invisible butler in *What the Butler Saw* as a stand-in for the cosy and complacent amenities of upper-middle-class drawing-room life. Incidentally, Orton saw a butler for the first time in his life on 24 January 1967, when he visited the Beatles, well after the first draft of this play was written (Lahr, p. 245).

Dr Prentice's establishment is actually a private lunatic asylum, which Orton fixes in his epigraph as a microcosm of the world: 'Surely we're all mad people, and they/Whom we think are, are not' (p. 361). By invoking Cyril Tourneur's Jacobean play, *The Revenger's Tragedy* (from about 1607), Orton is setting up as a model one of the strangest

and most extravagant of seventeenth-century black comedies, which is also a play much influenced by Shakespeare's *Hamlet*. It is a wildly, almost hysterically rhetorical
play that passes for tragedy only by certain technicalities of
the ending. Even better than *The Jew of Malta*, for which
T. S. Eliot coined the term 'tragic farce'. *The Revenger's
Tragedy* exemplifies all the bizarre and unanticipatable
shifts in tone that are associated with this paradoxical
genre. *What the Butler Saw* is hardly tragic – in fact, it is
close to *The Importance of Being Earnest* both in style and
plot (especially the lurid denouement) – but it plays with
large concepts of identity (particularly sexual identity),
incest, authority and maintaining one's sanity in a mad
world. These are all farcical themes with a certain natural
relevance to tragedy.

In his short book on Orton, C. W. E. Bigsby calls him 'the
high priest of farce in the mid-sixties' and points to his
development of a new kind of farce:

> But it was Orton's achievement to give farce a new
> meaning, to make it something more than the coy
> trysting with disorder it had once been. For Orton, farce
> became both an expression of anarchy and its only
> antidote. In his play, role playing is not a series of false
> surfaces concealing a real self; it is the total meaning or
> unmeaning of protagonists who survive by refusing all
> substance. (p. 17)

This is further defined in terms of entropy:

> The protagonists of this new farce-world are therefore
> themselves marginal, irrelevant to the slow unwinding of
> an entropic process, while the form itself is self-

destructive, implying the existence of no Platonic idea in the mad logic of its own configurations.   (p. 52)

This is a different kind of farce from the comfortable, domestic assumptions of Plautus's New Comedy, where all the formulae are worked out to produce the happy ending and perturbations are merely a plot device. In Aristophanes' Old Comedy, the endings generally celebrate the triumph of a splendid wish-fulfilment idea like peace, sexual bliss and the values of Cloud Cuckooland.

Orton's endings are sardonic. In *Entertaining Mr. Sloane*, the hoodlum picaro is, through murder, tamed into a bisexual stud forced to be shared between brother and sister. *Loot* ends with the bank robbers, the homicidal nurse, and the model detective from Scotland Yard parcelling out the loot among themselves, while the honest but pompous widower, Mr McLeavy, is conveniently framed and sent to prison. *What the Butler Saw* has an extraordinarily Dionysiac – or mock Dionysiac – ending, as Sergeant Match, clad only in the leopard-spotted dress of Mrs Prentice and the god Hercules, leads all the characters on stage to an apocalyptic exit through the skylight: '*They pick up their clothes and weary, bleeding, drugged and drunk, climb the rope ladder into the blazing light*' (p. 448). Lahr sees in the action a 'wink at Euripides' (p. 15), whose *Bacchae* was the inspiration for Orton's adult-camp farce, *The Erpingham Camp*.

In literature as in life, Orton was obsessed with the idea of comic festivity and celebration. Drawing on a distinction from Nietzsche's *Birth of Tragedy*, Orton elevates the values of comedy over those of tragedy:

I always say to myself that the theatre is the Temple of Dionysus, and not Apollo. You do the Dionysus thing on your typewriter, and then you allow a little Apollo in, just a little to shape and guide it along certain lines you may want to go along. But you can't allow Apollo in completely.

(Lahr, p. 15)

The Dionysiac enters *What the Butler Saw* through its enormous sexual energies. Orton recreates the raucous animal spirits of Aristophanes and Plautus rather than the refined bedroom farce of Feydeau. Polymorphous perversity is the guiding principle of Orton's play, and imaginative variety defines sexual value. The question of identity that is so crucial in tragedy is now translated into its farcical equivalent: sexual identity. The characters try vainly to establish their maleness or femaleness, only to discover that it hardly matters.

In the classic tradition of farce, transvestism is rampant, as if the costumes themselves were the only sure guide to the sexual identities of the characters. When Geraldine is dressed in the uniform of Nick, the bellhop of the Station Hotel, she cannot logically convince anyone that she is either a girl or a boy, and she floats frustratingly in that epicene middle state where the categories of masculine and feminine lose their clear outlines. This is definitely not bisexuality, but rather a comic release from the burdens of sexual identity. As an avowed homosexual, Orton could mercilessly twit both the gay and the straight worlds, and sexuality in his plays becomes a synonym for the imagination.

Dr Rance is the representative of the real world – 'Your immediate superiors in madness', as he puts it (p. 376) – but he is, of course, the most insane of all the characters in this private psychiatric clinic. His attempts at logic and common sense are the maddest thing about him, as he quizzes Geraldine on her sexual identity:

100

RANCE: Do you think of yourself as a girl?
GERALDINE: No.
RANCE: Why not?
GERALDINE: I'm a boy.
RANCE: (*kindly*). Do you have the evidence about you?
GERALDINE: (*her eyes flashing an appeal to* DR PRENTICE). I
    must be a boy. I like girls.
    DR RANCE *stops and wrinkles his brow, puzzled.*

(p. 413)

True to the spirit of farce, what is most obvious to the
audience is most hidden from the characters on stage, as Dr
Rance, by the conventions of the form, is forbidden to see
through even the simplest of the multitudinous disguises.

He cannot follow Geraldine's artlessly heterosexual
reasoning and, as a last resort, he insists on the evidence of
the senses:

RANCE: Take your trousers down. I'll tell you which sex
    you belong to.
GERALDINE: (*backing away*). I'd rather not know!
RANCE: You wish to remain in ignorance?
GERALDINE: Yes.
RANCE: I can't encourage you in such a self-indulgent
    attitude. You must face facts like the rest of us.

(p. 314)

But when, '*Provoked beyond endurance,* GERALDINE *flings
herself into* DR RANCE's *arms and cries hysterically* . . .
"Undress me then, doctor! Do whatever you like only
prove that I'm a girl"*', Dr Rance '*pushes away and turns,
frigidly to* DR PRENTICE' (p. 414). He recoils with horror
from the real life about which he is constantly talking.

Orton goes beyond classic farce to energise his play with
all possible varieties of sexual behaviour, buggery, nec-

101

rophilia, lesbianism, exhibitionism, hermaphroditism, rape, sadomasochism, fetishism, transvestism, nymphomania and the triumphant incest which crowns the mock-Wildean recognition scene. Orton is invoking the archly polished wit of Restoration comedy as it is refracted through Wilde's Victorian *rifacimento* of that style. Sex is entirely separated from guilt. With yeasty complications that multiply with alarming rapidity, sex symbolises the world of impulse on which comedy is based: at its heart it is dreamlike, self-gratifying, wish-fulfilling, and narcissistic. Thus, Mrs Prentice's exclamation, 'I want account taken of my sexual nature' (p. 234), is the real theme of the play, which seems to cure both her frigidity and her husband's impotence: the play itself acts out its own therapy.

Is Mrs Prentice a nyphomaniac? Hardly. Although Dr Prentice seems to think so, his wife is only dabbling in sex to entice him back to his marital duties. When she *'advances on* DR PRENTICE*'* with a gun, we have a homosexual's farcical hyperbole for the phallic woman attempting by force to seduce an unwilling male:

> MRS PRENTICE: (*waving the gun*). Come with me and lie down!
>
> PRENTICE: The woman is insatiable.
>
> MRS PRENTICE: Unless you make love to me I shall shoot you.
>
> PRENTICE: No husband can be expected to give his best at gun-point. (*Backing away.*)   (p. 436)

Throughout the play Mrs Prentice keeps encountering naked men that Dr Rance, with professional unction, assures her are a delusion. All this priapic and Dionysiac exhibitionism prepares Mrs Prentice for a sexual reconciliation with her husband:

DR PRENTICE *seizes her, smacks her face and tears the dress*
from her. She struggles.
MRS PRENTICE: (*gasping as he slaps her*). Oh, my darling!
This is the way to sexual adjustment in marriage.

(p. 431)

This mock sadomasochistic scenario is as close to sexual
fulfilment as the play ever comes.

Like Molière's Doctors (in *Le Médecin Malgré Lui*,
L'Amour Médecin and *Le Malade Imaginaire*), Orton's
psychiatrists in *What the Butler Saw* also represent an
arcane, technological system that has no relation to any
living reality; in other words, they are pious, jargonising,
mystifying, professional humbugs. Dr Rance – with a pun
on 'rants' – is the chief spokesman for psychiatric mumbo
jumbo, with Dr Prentice functioning as his apprentice. The
puns are self-consciously mischievous, and Orton is constantly doodling with wordplay, especially the double
entendres and sexual euphemisms of British popular
speech like 'service' (pp. 390, 445), 'disturb' (p. 396),
'interfere' (p. 408), and 'misbehave' (p. 443). In the spirit
of David Lodge's *The British Museum Is Falling Down*
(1965), Mrs Prentice is said to be 'harder to get into than
the reading room at the British Museum' (p. 396).

Like *Hamlet*, the whole play turns on the question of the
missing father, as in the very first exchange between Dr
Prentice and Geraldine: 'Who was your father?' (p. 363).
To spectators schooled in melodrama, this question dis-
closes that incest will be the central theme, a point that
Rance belabours with uncanny foresight. Rance is the
coldly theoretical observer, the authority figure, whose
speculations lie outside the ascertainable facts of the play.
Almost immediately upon seeing the naked Geraldine, he
certifies her as insane and prepares to admit her as a

patient. There is no way of interrupting the barrage of psychoanalytic babble by which Rance hypothesises her case. The questions require no answers, and we are snugly ensconced in the black comedy world of Joseph Heller's *Catch 22* (which has similar psychiatric interviews):

RANCE: Who was the first man in your life?

GERALDINE: My father.

RANCE: Did he assault you?

GERALDINE: No!

RANCE: (*to* DR PRENTICE). She may mean 'Yes' when she says 'No'. It's elementary feminine psychology. (*To* GERALDINE.) Was your step-mother aware of your love for your father?

GERALDINE: I lived in a normal family. I had no love for my father.

RANCE: (*to* DR PRENTICE). I'd take a bet that she was the victim of an incestuous attack. She clearly associates violence and the sexual act. Her attempt, when naked, to provoke you to erotic response may have deeper significance. (p. 382)

Like Freud, Dr Rance wants to displace the 'erotic response' on to some 'deeper significance' and not regard it directly as a sexual expression. So we wind up with the farcical displacement of reality, by which all literal meanings and truths disappear and everything means something else.

Orton saw psychiatry as a mad system of pseudo-meanings, a way of suffocating experience in language that has no relation to any perceivable reality. On 9 June 1967, he said in an interview in the *Evening News*: 'Everybody is a little like psychiatrists today. They've got this enormous wish to explain everything. Religion – especially Christianity – tries to show things following a logical progression. And for all we know the whole thing may turn out to be some vast joke' (Lahr, p. 261). In Dr Rance's world, sexuality as primitive impulse disappears to be replaced by myth-making and fictionalising. It looks as if Dr Rance's chief function in the play is to gather materials for a lurid best seller:

> The ugly shadow of anti-Christ stalks this house. Having discovered her Father/Lover in Dr Prentice the patient replaces him in a psychological reshuffle by that archetypal Father-figure – the Devil himself. Everything is now clear. The final chapters of my book are knitting together: incest, buggery, outrageous women and strange love-cults catering for depraved appetites. All the fashionable bric-à-brac. (p. 427)

Like Stoppard, Orton delights in the merging of fiction into reality and the conversion of one into the other. By the logic of New Farce, the play proper has stopped and Dr Rance is doing his turn, a little set piece exhibiting the 'growing menace of pornography', on which he is determined to cash in. We are in the self-conscious, metatheatrical world of artifice and literature as Dr Rance rises to his moral peroration: 'The whole treacherous avant-garde movement will be exposed for what it is – an instrument for inciting decent citizens to commit bizarre crimes against humanity and the state!' (p. 428). This is like Orton's obscenely moralising letters that he wrote under the name of Mrs Edna[1] Welthorpe, including a scathing attack on his own play *Entertaining Mr. Sloane* (printed in the Letters to the Editor column of the *Daily Telegraph*):

I myself was nauseated by this endless parade of mental

and physical perversion. And to be told that such a disgusting piece of filth now passes for humour.

Today's young playwrights take it upon themselves to flaunt their contempt for ordinary decent people. I hope that the ordinary decent people will shortly strike *back*!

(Lahr, pp. 166–7)

Thus Rance delights in the lurid denouement of *What the Butler Saw*, with its split elephant brooch and sentimental memories of a rape in the linen cupboard on the second floor of the Station Hotel during a blackout: 'Double incest is even more likely to produce a best-seller than murder – and this is as it should be for love *must* bring greater joy than violence' (p. 446).

Is this the final meaning of Orton's farce, that 'love *must* bring greater joy than violence'? In some way the climax of *What the Butler Saw* is a structural device for transforming violence into love. The play ends '*in a great blaze of glory*' (p. 446), as the characters embrace one another and prepare for their ritual ascent on the rope ladder through the skylight. Dr Rance, the inquisitorial inspector-general of psychiatry, is revealed as the author-in-the-play, who was not only seeking out enormities, but also trying to create them for the sake of his steamy novel. He is disarmed by his own fictions. Sexual fulfilment awaits all these '*bleeding, drugged and drunk*' characters, weary and sore, as they wend their naked ways to a heaven of polymorphously perverse indulgences. The ending is wonderfully satisfying, but ironic. Can the power of Winston Churchill's phallus, waved triumphantly over the celebrants, bring eternal happiness? As Mrs Prentice says in another connection: 'the pleasures of the senses quickly pall' (p. 431); and as Geraldine explains very near the end: 'I'm a patient. I'm telling the truth!' We need especially to heed Dr Rance's wise answer: 'It's much too late to tell the truth' (p. 437). Orton establishes his credentials as a dramatist far beyond mere truth-telling.

In Orton's brief and meteoric career we see the playwright struggling with a characteristically modern problem: how to make literature out of life, but also how to disentangle literature and life so that one is not an abrasive simulacrum for the other – in other words, how to escape from the trap of autobiography. Orton's solution in his earlier plays, especially *Entertaining Mr. Sloane* and *Loot*, was to distance the events of his life by a blank, occulted, Pinteresque style. The characters are all menacing masks with an uncomfortable relation to Orton's unloving, coquettish mother; his ineffectual, horticultural father; and the dramatist himself in his ruffian/poet guise – there is an unacknowledged debt to the personae of Tennessee Williams.

What the Butler Saw, Orton's last play, is a new departure, and it represents a way out of the problems both of autobiography and of the heavy indebtedness to Pinter. By writing a farce, Orton is able to mute the large significances of his earlier work and to distance any intrusive sense of propinquity either to his own life or to his literary models, especially Pinter. As a genre, farce lends itself to depersonalisation and to the ritual enactment of the values of comedy. Saturnalia replaces satire, and the wish fulfilment of polymorphous perversity, both in sex and in language, is vigorously celebrated. In *What the Butler Saw* Orton manages to combine, with brilliance and originality, the virtues of Old and New Farce. There is the tumultuous sexual energy of Aristophanes, the careful intrigue plotting of Plautus, and the self-conscious, parodic, histrionic clowning of modern black comedy in the style of Beckett, Pinter, Ionesco, Stoppard, and especially Brecht.

We know from Lahr's incisive biography that Orton read much more widely than is generally believed, and he had a literate sense of his own place in the history of stage comedy. He was most conscious of his relation to Wilde, whom he admired for taking 'great pains' with his work (Lahr, p. 202), but whom he faulted for being 'flabby and self-indulgent' in his life (Lahr, p. 126). In a review of *Loot* in the *Observer*, Ronald Bryden cleverly labelled Orton the 'Oscar Wilde of Welfare State gentility'. He always wanted 'to write a play as good as *The Importance of Being Earnest*',[2] but Orton the body-builder and physical culturist admired Wilde and Congreve for some very surprising qualities:

> Oscar Wilde's style is much more earthy and colloquial than most people notice. When we look at Lady Brack-nell, she's the most ordinary, common, direct woman; she's not an affected woman at all. People are taken in by 'the glittering style'. It's not glitter. Congreve is the same. It's real – a slice of life. It's just very brilliantly written, perfectly believable. Nothing at all incredible.
>
> (Lahr, pp. 106–7)

This is exactly the criterion Orton held up for farce. In response to a wretchedly arty production of Feydeau's *A Flea in Her Ear*, Orton insisted that 'in Farce everything (the externals) must be believed' (Lahr, p. 143). Without this core of credibility, the farce would degenerate into meaningless and chaotic motion without any purpose. Orton plays with a concept of reality strongly enunciated in Lewis Carroll's *Through the Looking-Glass*:

> 'I *am* real! said Alice, and began to cry. . . .
> 'If I wasn't real,' Alice said – half laughing through her

108

tears, it all seemed so ridiculous – I shouldn't be able to cry.'
'I hope you don't suppose those are *real* tears?' Tweedledum interrupted in a tone of great contempt.[3]

To Mrs Prentice's desperate question, 'Is this blood real?' (showing her hands), Tweedledum Rance of course answers 'No' (p. 439), and when Nick is shot in the shoulder, presumably by Rance, he confronts the psychiatrist's vapid fictionalising with pain and blood:

NICK: I can't be an hallucination. (*He points to his bleeding shoulder*.) Look at this wound. That's real.
RANCE: It appears to be.
NICK: If the pain is real I must be real.
RANCE: I'd rather not get involved in metaphysical speculation.

(p. 443)

The bleeding Mrs Prentice, Nick and Sergeant Match challenge the impunity rule of traditional farce. In the mock-triumphant ending of the play, the characters are nevertheless *'weary, bleeding, drugged and drunk'* (p. 448).

In what sense can farce be 'real – a slice of life', 'perfectly believable'? The point of New Farce as one finds it in Ionesco and Stoppard and Orton is to uphold the old Ciceronian ideal that comedy should be an image of the world, a mirror of manners, and a model for how the rational man can conduct his life in an irrational world. Even though less overt than *Entertaining Mr. Sloane* and *Loot*, *What the Butler Saw* is still a bitter indictment of a world gone mad. Like Wilde, Orton did not make any tedious and artificial distinctions between earnestness and levity. Orton thought of himself as a very traditional and moral exponent of the well-made play, and it is Rance, the inspector-general who comes from afar, who speaks the final words of the piece, an affirmation of the reality principle: 'I'm glad you don't despise tradition. Let us put our clothes on and face the world' (p. 448).

8
Farce and Panic in 'Up Against It'

In 1967, the last year of his life, Orton had completed the first draft of *What the Butler Saw* and had sold the Broadway rights to *Loot* when he was asked by Walter Shenson to do a screenplay for the Beatles. It was a moment of great exhilaration in Orton's career. What was intended as a rewrite of an old script already commissioned by the Beatles turned into an entirely new project. The boldness and zaniness of *Up Against It* was obviously unsuitable for the respectable public image of the Beatles, and the script, which Orton put together in a few weeks, was eventually rejected, probably at the behest of Brian Epstein, the Beatles' manager. Although Oscar Lewenstein bought it almost at once, *Up Against It* was much revised and rewritten but never produced. In its present form it seems like a brilliant first draft that needs to be worked out and made fully cinematic. Orton's descriptions of camera shots

111

are more literary than cinematic – more like the epic descriptions on Brechtian banners.

It is a pity that Orton and the Beatles never pooled their Dionysiac energies since *Up Against It* is a more vivacious, audacious and original farce than anything the Beatles had ever done. *A Hard Day's Night*, *Help* and even *The Yellow Submarine* seem tame and respectable by comparison. Although *Up Against It* draws on the plot and characters of Orton's early novel, *Head to Toe* (1971), its epigrammatic style and teasing absurdity are in the spirit of *What the Butler Saw*, which Orton had just finished writing. The gynaecocracy of *Head to Toe*, with Connie as Chief of Police and the intensely feminine Lillian Corbett as Prime Minister (who is soon assassinated), reappears in *Up Against It*, along with revolution, prison scenes, and strangely ubiquitous characters like Bernard Coates and the Fat Man in the hole, but the sardonic, philosophising mood of Orton's early novel has disappeared. Instead we are firmly planted in the world of farce where anything can happen. The characters in *Up Against It* specialise in romantic platitudes and their ironic reversals. When Ian McTurk at the end finally forswears his Rowena for the '*kind, rather plain*' (p. 1) Miss Drumgoole, he confesses with some temerity: 'My heart is broken, but everything else is in working order' (p. 68). Our last vision in the film is the ecstatic Miss Drumgoole with her three new husbands. As Orton explains in his notes:

Already have the idea that the end should be a church with four bridegrooms and one bride. THE HOMECOMING [by Pinter] in fact, but alibied in such a way that no one could object. Lots of opportunities for sexual ambiguities. . . . (p. vi)

Unlimited sexual opportunity is only one of the links with *What the Butler Saw*. The polymorphous perversity celebrated in that play also endows *Up Against It* with a wonderful sense of anarchic freedom. It is as if all sexuality is seen freshly from outside, and the homosexual camp of Orton's script is by no means an apology for the gay life style. As in Feydeau, we are kept aware of a dazzling number of items in the sexual inventory, especially trousers, the absence of which is always a commitment to sex. When Bernard Coates appears in the hall of Money-Box Lodge, Mrs O'Scullion reminds him of homosexual proprieties: 'Why are you talking to strange young men without your trousers?' (p. 16). She remains unconvinced by Coates's explanation: 'It was premature to take your clothes off. He's obviously a burglar.' The same vaudeville/music hall routines are worked again on the theme of showers. When Rowena, the most modern of women, invites Ian McTurk to shower with her, Ramsay '*looks shocked*': 'We can't take a shower with you. You're a woman.' The artful Rowena understands this in a special sense: 'Would you like to take one with my husband [Bernard Coates again]? I'll call him. He'll be delighted to oblige' (p. 43). Later when Ian McTurk is prepared to give Rowena 'a good raping' in her cabin, the subject of showers comes up again in what is a typically patterned and logically absurd dialogue:

ROWENA: We shouldn't be doing this. Think of my husband.

MCTURK: I wish you wouldn't keep harping on your husband. I took a shower with him yesterday. What more do you want? (p. 47)

McTurk's sexual ambiguity gives a special edge to the

113

romantic clichés on which *Up Against It* is based. Homosexual camp sets all sexuality askew.

We must, of course, agree that 'Any well-regulated society must find room for anti-social activity' (p. 63), but beyond these liberal shibboleths the norm keeps slipping away. The accepted, heterosexual, bourgeois world is topsy-turvy, so that Ramsay can express astonishment at what is most obvious and proper: 'Getting married and having children is the most rebellious thing a man can do. It shows a disregard for the conventional bourgeois status-quo and a fine, careless anarchic sense of the absurd' (p. 68). But this easy reversal of sexual norms itself illustrates Orton's own 'fine, careless anarchic sense of the absurd'. This is a comic ideal.

Orton's campiness is consistently anti-heroic and deflating. Everything has a prosaic explanation. Thus, when the inflamed Rowena in her cabin is both fighting off and encouraging Ian McTurk, the Lustful Turk, she *'gives a cry of horror'* when her lover of long ago (who has, in fact, had her virginity) takes off his shirt: 'What are those scars on your back? Are they the marks of the lash?' Slightly kinky? 'No. I've been wearing an overtight string vest' (p. 48). The lash and the overtight string vest are both part of a lurid, popular culture image of sex that Orton never tired of twitting. These images are, of course, the other side of the genteel posturing that Orton found so offensive in British respectability. They are the sort of things that Orton, under the persona of Mrs Edna Welthorpe, delighted in excoriating.

The transvestite humour of Ramsay, McTurk and Low disguised as women in order to assassinate the Prime Minister is designed to titillate a middle-class audience. *'With heavily made-up eyes, furs and smart hats, they resemble perfectly women of authority and fashion'* (p. 26).

'We're perfectly respectable girls', says Ramsay, who claims to represent 'the nice part of Acton' (p. 26), and McTurk extravagantly cites his auntie as 'the spiritual adviser to a baking powder firm'. Before the Prime Minister is assassinated, she announces a decision 'that is sure to have far-reaching consequences': 'We're having the House of Commons redecorated in Chinese white lacquer and natural oak woodwork!' (p. 29). The tawdry cheapness of the stage direction that follows is Busby Berkeley and Rocky Horror Show combined: '*Every woman in the hall gives an exclamation of delight. A shimmer of silk, a sway of feathers, the tinkling of ten thousand pearls*' (p. 29). Pearls only tinkle in Hollywood musicals.

Up Against It is heavily drenched in romantic clichés, all of which are rendered self-consciously absurd. Lust and aggression – or at least grotesque misunderstandings – lurk close to the surface in the most artfully embellished scenes. Thus Rowena and McTurk play out their sentimental attachment in a setting that seems to frustrate their ardour. Scene 34 is The Rose Arbour: '*They embrace in the centre of the arbour. He kisses her. Rose petals, each one touched with a pearl of dew, fall slowly upon them*' (p. 17). Later '*The arbour swings away from* McTURK. *The colours dissolve. The shadows reach out to him. He clings to* ROWENA' (p. 18). We remember that in the production notes Orton said that 'colour is used as a weapon' (Lahr, p. 250). McTurk is the mooning romantic lead but Rowena is arch:

MCTURK: I never want to leave you again. We'll be together forever.
ROWENA: (*with a tinkly laugh*). Of course we will. Only this morning I'm playing tennis. So you will excuse me, won't you? (p. 18)

Her tinkly laugh is like the tinkling of ten thousand pearls because Rowena is 'destined for richer hands' than McTurk's.

The rose arbour reappears in Scene 121, which is set in a moonlit garden: *'Dark leaves. Roses. A nightingale. Faintly blown by the wind comes the sound of a waltz'* (p. 64). Rowena is always an exemplar of profitable common sense: 'I must go! Love seems out of place in a garden in the moonlight.' But the scene nevertheless ends with a romantic flourish: *'Petals from a rose fall softly upon them from an overhanging bough. The moonlight folds them in a shining embrace as they kiss before parting forever'* (p. 65). In good Wildean fashion, 'in matters of grave importance, style, not sincerity, is the vital thing'. Orton delights in frustrating our comfortable expectations and the flowered rhetoric runs counter to the sardonic intent.

Orton's epigrammatic style freezes the dialogue in a perfectly patterned frame. Generally the epigrams reverse our conventional anticipations, but they also convey a sense of comic licence; in other words, the playwright can stop the action as he chooses for the sake of polished wit. All the epigrams seem slightly off and therefore encourage a feeling of black comedy uneasiness in the audience. The most quoted line in *Up Against It* is undoubtedly McTurk's apothegm: 'Anything that is worth doing is worth doing in public' (p. 34). In context the revolutionaries are attacking the privacy and secrecy of the gynaecocracy they have overthrown: 'We'll pass a law forbidding anyone to entertain in private. We cannot afford this stifling secrecy' (p. 34). Does McTurk's line mean that anything that cannot be done in public is not worth doing, or does he imply that in the new regime all shame and restraint will disappear and that everything can be done openly? The ambiguity is teasing, but I think Orton cultivates this kind of uncertain

response. When the distraught Low enters Money-Box
Lodge, Mrs O'Scullion points a gun at him. Low protests:
'I'm hungry and thirsty. I need help', but the Mayor's Wife
cuts off any sentimentality: 'I'm not interested in your
private life' (p. 16). Is this part of the same equation that
'Anything that is worth doing is worth doing in public'?
Clearly hunger and thirst are not worth doing at all and are
therefore part of a mythical private life that Mrs O'Scullion
has excluded from her consideration. There is a Marxist
bite in Orton's drawing-room frivolity.

Up Against It does not lack frivolity but it is usually of a
puzzling sort. What are we to make of the exchange
between Low and McTurk?

LOW: Is there any woman you wouldn't wait in the rain
for?

McTURK: The Statue of Liberty.   (p. 6)

Why the Statue of Liberty and just what kind of nonsense
are we dealing with? Thus Rowena is sent to a convent in
which 'All the nuns are women' (p. 6), McTurk as prisoner is
denied the right of appeal because of his height – 'You're
too small to lodge an appeal' (p. 38) – and Coates has bad
teeth 'because if you're rich it doesn't matter whether you
disgust people or not. In fact I'll go as far as to say that the
poor prefer the rich to be disgusting' (p. 13). There is a
certain lacerating quality in these witty reversals of normal
expectations. This is not a movie in which the Beatles could
have comfortably represented the accepted values of the
counter-culture. They would certainly have baffled their
trusted audience with *Up Against It*. Accused of taking the
virginity of Rowena, who was seen to enter McTurk's room
'in an advanced state of nudity' (p. 4), McTurk protests:
'Nobody is provocative at four in the morning', which is

117

itself a provocative remark. Obviously McTurk does not
require provocation, and he has 'left the blind up as well.
. . . The last indulgence of a sensualist' (p. 4). We are
already well on our way to the climactic dictum: 'Anything
that is worth doing is worth doing in public.'

How are we to understand the fun in *Up Against It*?
Throughout his life Orton was inordinately fond of anarchy
and mayhem, acts of spontaneous terror that threatened
the cosy assumptions of daily life. The homosexual saturnalia in men's toilets that are so vividly recorded in his
diaries are one bright example, and another is the scenes in
the Islington public libraries when Orton and Halliwell
returned their doctored books and stayed to watch the
expressions of horror on the faces of the prim old ladies
who encountered the obscene book jackets and blurbs.

Scene 116 of *Up Against It* is a farcical and apocalyptic
battle in which everything is destroyed in a series of ever
more grandiose gestures. The action begins with an ambul-
ance crashing into a lorry. Then two ambulances are blown
up by a mine and the same injured and horrified soldiers
keep being passed to a series of new stretcher-bearers. As
the ambulances and stretcher-bearers escalate, a hole
suddenly opens in the earth and swallows them up. It is near
this point that the '*shocked, injured and well-nigh senseless*'
(p. 61) McTurk, Ramsay and Low decline to be helped and
fight off the stretcher-bearers. When Father Brodie suddenly appears '*holding high the* CROSS *upon which* OUR LORD
died, accompanied by NUNS *and* CHOIR BOYS *singing a Hymn
to the Glory of Immortal God*' (p. 62) – an epiphany right
out of Orton's *The Erpingham Camp* – Ramsay reacts in a
way that brings farce and panic very close together: he
'*shrieks with maniacal laughter and begins to leap about in a
kind of glee*' (p. 62). The scene has all the ingredients of the
obligatory chase at the end of many early American film

comedies, in which the number of vehicles, the involvement of all bystanders, the pace, and the frenzy were mercilessly accelerated until the anti-climactic climax could still the furor. The comic format is that of the endlessly proliferated shaggy-dog story.

Orton delighted in making fun of his own art, and he took especial pleasure in writing *Up Against It*, which he considered a trivial project in which he could freely borrow material from *Entertaining Mr. Sloane*, *Loot*, *Head to Toe*, and other early novels. But the first draft of the film script is a much more exuberant and original work than Orton may have realised. One additional ingredient is the parody of old movies and especially the conventions of romantic melodrama. The plot of *Up Against It* is much wilder than any of Orton's plays, which are always thoroughly well made. Orton did not forgive Pinter all of his loose ends in plotting. The looser form of the film script allows Orton licence to move around freely without worrying about the consequences for plot and character.

Thus Ramsay's father keeps popping up in odd places, and, of course, he turns out to be an impostor:

MCTURK: Is that old man really your father?
RAMSAY: No. But I allow him to think he is.
MCTURK: Why?
RAMSAY: There's no time to explain.   (p. 23)

The pseudonymous and spurious father obviously has deep roots in Orton's psyche, and Ramsay's father is the archetypal political hack out of the mob in Shakespeare's *Julius Caesar*. Like many of Orton's more important characters, he is almost totally devoid of ideology:

OLD MAN: Freedom from tyranny!

119

MCTURK: (*with interest*). Are you oppressed?

OLD MAN: No.

MCTURK: Then why are you calling for freedom?

OLD MAN: I always do at these meetings. I've been coming
   to them all my life. (*He waves a flag.*) Death to the
   oppressors! (p. 22)

This is all chillingly political or apolitical, and Orton
delights in the meaningless significant event.

McTurk's own father 'was strangled during a political
disturbance'. Miss Drumgoole asks innocently: 'Was he
demonstrating against the Government?' 'No', answers the
son, 'He was selling fruit to passing tourists' (p. 19). This is
a snappy music hall routine. McTurk's mother was dogged
by bad luck, as exemplified by the fact that 'She threw
herself over the balcony of a cinema during a Mario Lanza
film' (p. 19). Cheapness again, and Orton is a master of the
sleazy and the third-rate. Why Mario Lanza as martyr-
maker? The final portentous nonsense of the film script is
spoken by Ramsay's putative father, who moves easily
from Field Marshal to hotel page, since the uniform is the
same: 'Everything's in a state of flux. (*He shakes his head,
coughs a little.*) We live in an era of constant change and
extreme conservatism' (p. 70). We remember that the
denouement of *What the Butler Saw* also depends upon
crucial events that occur in a hotel. In *Up Against It* the very
last scene takes place in a hotel bedroom with the sun
streaming in as Miss Drumgoole '*squeals with delight and
disappears under the coverlet with her husbands*' (p. 70).
What more could we want from the Beatles' great unmade
movie – perhaps only that there be four young men in the
bed instead of three.

Orton had a genius for pop art images that enshrine a
sense of wistful absurdity. He could capture the meaning-

less gesture that is entirely characteristic, which is probably why there is a growing interest in his small body of work more than fifteen years after his death. No modern dramatist has such a powerful, almost mythical reputation with such a slight *oeuvre*, and we are beginning to understand how different Orton's achievement is from Pinter's. One brilliant touch that is worth dwelling on occurs in Scene 87 in McTurk's prison cell, an episode that is considerably compressed from the endless prison scenes in *Head to Toe*. The passage of time is marked by the pin-up girl on McTurk's calendar. She begins as '*a young girl in the briefest of bikinis*' posed with a beach ball. As time moves on '*The girl on the calendar grows older. From being a lovely seventeen-year-old she matures into a ripe twenty-seven.*' She is then thirty-seven and at the end she is '*old, grey-haired, withered. She still holds up the beach ball with a gay smile. She has no teeth. Her smile is hideous*' (p. 39). The time, of course, is surrealistically measured, since McTurk is still a young man when he escapes from prison, but the changes in the calendar girl are a farcical rendition of McTurk's growing up.

He learns nothing from experience at all except that romance is systematically frustrated. Rowena slips into richer hands and McTurk must eventually share the very plain Miss Drumgoole with Low and Ramsay. The rhapsodic ending in bright sunlight promises a heaven of polymorphously perverse delights. It is a perfect Orton irony for the best of all possible worlds. In an earlier exchange McTurk and Miss Drumgoole are seen to be separated from each other with finality:

McTURK: Are you enjoying yourself?
MISS DRUMGOOLE: No. I'd rather be married to you.
McTURK: That's impossible. My heart is broken.   (p. 45)

By the time of the happy ending which cures all ills, McTurk's heart is still broken, but he proposes to Miss Drumgoole and is accepted (along with his friends, Ramsay and Low). This is as close as Orton comes to comic acknowledgement of the fallen world, the end of innocence, and the loss of romance.

9
Conclusion: The Ortonesque

A few weeks before his death on 9 August 1967, Orton had finished typing a new version of *What the Butler Saw*, and he was getting ready for his next play, tentatively called *Prick Up Your Ears*. It was to be an 'historical farce set on the eve of Edward VII's coronation in 1902'. Orton already had an excellent epigraph from Sheridan's *The Critic*: 'Where history gives you a good heroic outline for a play, you may fill up with a little love at your own discretion: in doing which, nine times out of ten, you only make up a deficiency in the private history of the times' (Lahr, p. 22). Orton's Edwardian play was never written, so he never managed to fill it up with a little love at his own discretion. The artifice of the Edwardian era appealed to Orton, since it offered the possibility of reviving the Restoration comedy of manners, as practised by Congreve, Wycherley, Etherege, and others. Orton was alert to manners, and the appropriate style accompanying them, as a mask for morals. This was his most fundamental irony because the vulgarity, greed and lust of his characters are always

123

peeping through no matter how elegantly they express themselves.

At the time Orton was devising *Prick Up Your Ears*, he was also thinking of amusing himself 'by writing a bit of rubbish under an assumed name: in the nature of a joke play' (Lahr, p. 256). And it is under an assumed name, Mrs Edna Welthorpe, that Orton requests permission from the Heath Street Baptist Church Hall to begin rehearsals of *The Pansy*, 'a play which pleads for greater tolerance on the subject of homosexuality' (Lahr, p. 115). Later, under the aegis of the secretary of the Phallus Players, Orton apologises for the rudeness of his late niece, Edna. *The Pansy* is obviously a later version of *The Decapitated Pansy*, a stray title from Orton's notebooks. This appears among a provocative list that includes *Strange Pedicure*, *The Painted Whip*, *A Stag for Nanny* and *A Cow Called Isis* (Lahr, p. 106). These resemble the plays Orton attributed to Emlyn Williams in the doctored Islington Library copy of volume one of Williams' collected works: *Knickers Must Fall*, *Up the Front*, *Up the Back*, *Olivia Prude*, *He Was Born Grey*, *Mr. Winifred* and *Fucked by Monty* (Lahr, p. 81). It is obvious that Orton thought of writing as a form of play. He delighted in mystifications, send-ups and put-ons, and considered himself as an entertainer both in the theatre and in life. He was, in his own words, 'the fly on the wall', a gadfly of the human comedy.

How, finally, can we describe Orton's achievement in the theatre or define what we mean by the Ortonesque? It is a peculiar mixture of farce and viciousness, especially as it expresses itself in the greed, lust and aggression that lie just beneath the surface of British middle-class proprieties. Orton never tired of ridiculing the public language and public morality of the corporate, welfare state. Lahr defines the Ortonesque as 'a shorthand adjective for scenes of macabre outrageousness' (p. 5). The outrageousness is a form of panic among the complacent, the self-satisfied, the pampered and the overfed. Through laughter and comic purgation, farce offers a way of disturbing audiences. As Eric Bentley and Barbara Freedman explain the genre,[1] farce insulates us from the wild aggression that is so energetically aroused. We are convinced that it will all come out well in the end. But in the black comedy version of farce the cushioning against injury and loss is not so secure as it is in the farces of Plautus and Feydeau. The plays of Orton are not as merry as their plots would suggest; in fact, they leave us with an unpleasant sense of a world gone awry. They are disorienting and distasteful for audiences and critics alike, who sometimes cry out in distress at having been duped – in other words, of not getting the frivolous, light-hearted, knickers farce they were promised.

In his style, Orton was searching for a 'combination of elegance and crudity', which 'is always ridiculous' (Lahr, p. 135). This was a remark occasioned by his reading of Genet's *Querelle of Brest*, and Orton found the humourless Genet 'the most perfect example of an unconscious humorist at work since Marie Corelli'. A combination of elegance and crudity depends upon a strong incongruity between social class and style. Orton's characters always speak in a highly mannered, self-conscious and artificial mode, as if they were knowingly characters in a play. Their mostly crude, lower-class origins are veiled by elegant, patterned, even epigrammatic speech. In this respect Orton learned a great deal from Firbank about how to mask social distinctions and class consciousness by having his characters speak a language that is highly formalised and embellished but has little or no overt content. The dialogue in an Orton play is generally a string of conventionalised social gestures that say nothing directly. What is happening in the play has nothing to do with what the characters are telling each other; in fact, speech offers a way of obfuscating or 'occulting' the real thoughts and feelings of the characters.

Orton flaunted his lower-class, Leicester background and made no attempt whatsoever to pass. His diaries record his Dionysian, picaresque, sexual adventures in men's lavatories, which Orton used to explode middle-class respectability. The sexual and the social merge, for example, in the 'little pissoir under the bridge', which suddenly becomes 'the scene of a frenzied saturnalia. No more than two feet away the citizens of Holloway moved about their ordinary business' (Lahr, p. 233). These spontaneous eruptions of the theatrical into ordinary life were a form of adventure that Orton actively sought, especially in the rough trade of chance homosexual encounters. There is an amusing autobiographical touch in *What the Butler Saw* when Mrs Prentice reveals to Dr Rance that her husband has been secretly writing letters to newspapers: in his latest 'he calls Gentlemen's Lavatories "the last stronghold of male privilege . . ." ' (p. 388).

Orton was preoccupied with vulgarity in his plays. All of his most vigorous characters are vulgar in the literal sense of the term: they pretend to a refinement, tact and gentility that they do not at all have. Their politeness consists of empty, conventionalised formulae – slogans, proverbs, advertising copy, political shibboleths, and all the other verbal junk of a liberal, democratic society. In *Entertaining Mr. Sloane*, for example, the thuggish Ed is constantly alluding to his 'principles'. After Sloane's murder of Ed's old father, Ed finds it more than easy to indulge himself in the tedious pietisms of a benevolent society:

You're completely without morals, boy. I hadn't realized

how depraved you were. You murder my father. Now
you ask me to help you evade Justice. Is that where my
liberal principles have brought me?   (p. 134)

For once in the play, Sloane is at bay and has to speak the
truth: 'You've got no principles'. But Ed's smug speechify-
ing is not to be stopped by anything so superficial as the
truth:

> No principles? Oh, you really have upset me now. Why
> am I interested in your welfare? Why did I give you a
> job? Why do thinking men everywhere show young boys
> the straight and narrow? Flash cheque-books when
> delinquency is mentioned? Support the Scout-
> movement? Principles, boy, bleeding principles. And
> don't you dare say otherwise or you'll land in serious
> trouble.

The last line is a thinly veiled threat in the style of
Inspector Truscott of *Loot*, but Sloane knows how to
provide for himself:

> SLOANE: (*sits beside* ED. *Lays a hand on his knee*). I accept
>   responsibility.
> ED: Do you?
> SLOANE: Fully.
> ED: Good. Remove that hand, will you?   (p. 135)

Sloane finally accommodates himself to Ed's rhetoric when
he confesses: 'I'm very bad. Only you can help me on the
road to a useful life.' The language is that of soap opera, but
the real meaning is insidious.
    Orton had no ambiguities at all about what Sloane and

Eddie represent. In a letter to Alan Schneider, the American director of the play, Orton says:

> Sloane knows Eddie wants him. He has absolutely no qualms about surrendering his body. None. He's done it many, many times. Sloane is no virgin. . . . But he isn't going to give in until he has to. . . . Eddie, naturally, doesn't know how amoral Sloane is. He imagines that he has a virgin on his hands. He thinks he can get Sloane. Sure he can. But it may take a bit of time – cause Sloane is such a nice kid. (Lahr, p. 148)

This comment has surprisingly little to do with the overt dialogue of the play; rather it is part of the game of hide-and-seek that Sloane and Eddie are playing with each other. Ed is clearly a muscular Christian, into sports, the military and leather. His interrogation of Sloane is a curious mixture of S&M and YMCA:

> ED: Do you wear leather . . . next to the skin? leather jeans, say? Without . . . aah . . .
> SLOANE: Pants?
> ED: (*laughs*). Get away! (*Pause.*) The question is are you clean living? You may as well know I set great store by morals. (p. 87)

Ed is teasing himself with erotic suggestions. *Entertaining Mr. Sloane* puts heavy emphasis on its sexual subtext, with the characters always trying to cover what they are actually doing in genteel platitudes.

Orton's television play, *The Good and Faithful Servant*, offers a useful contrast with *Entertaining Mr. Sloane* because, in its attempt to indict a cruel, heartless and depersonalising industrial society, it is hardly Ortonesque at all. Except in the character of Ray, the farce breaks down and emotions are directly engaged. This is the only play by Orton in which pathos plays an important role. The party at the Bright Hours Club for retired employees in Scene 16 is so sad that we lose all sense of comic displacement. It opens with a number of old ex-employees singing around an upright piano: 'We'll All Go Riding on a Rainbow to a New Land Far Away'. The voices are described as '*Weary, apathetic*' (p. 183), and the scene ends with the singing of 'all songs with "Happy" in them' (p. 189). In between, an old woman at the end of the room falls over and dies, and the one person who seems to know Buchanan is mistaken. The high point of Buchanan's career is when his photo appeared in the firm's magazine, and the old man who is with him, the skittles expert, reached the apex of his fame when he 'was almost mentioned in a well-known sporting periodical' (p. 185). Meanwhile, among the other characters in this scene, '*Two of them are in wheelchairs, one is blind, a couple are simple-minded. They stare at* BUCHANAN *without interest*' (p. 184). The detail is excruciatingly cruel in a way that is uncharacteristic of Orton. We expect that farce will distance the pain and that the characters will be comically insulated from real life. Scene 16 of *The Good and Faithful Servant* is grotesque, believable, and moving in a way that works against the comic effect.

Orton usually thought of farce as very close to tragedy. He describes *Loot* as taking 'a farcical view of things normally treated as tragic', and Shakespeare's tragedies, if played plain, 'are nearly farcical. All gradations of theatre between tragedy and farce – light comedy, drama – are a load of rubbish' (Lahr, pp. 186–7). The mistake of *The Good and Faithful Servant* is that it tries to be tragic without first being farcical. In this sense it violates the canons of the Ortonesque, which demand a more oblique and occulted approach. Above all, Orton hated cant, solemnity and seriousness. The significance of *Loot*, for example, has to emerge from the farce, to transcend it: 'There's supposed to be a healthy shock, for instance, at those moments in *Loot* when an audience suddenly *stops* laughing' (Lahr, p. 187). This is the essence of black comedy.

Orton considered himself a *poète maudit* like Rimbaud, fated to be out of touch with his public and to die young. He tried to live out the myth of celebrity, speaking in the synthetic, artful and jokey language of a character in his own plays. Events seemed to be whirling out of his grasp. His death was histrionic in the extreme, a media event, and people who knew nothing about his life and even less about his works lapped up the details of his murder with avid glee. He was the new Chatterton, the marvellous boy, the archetype of the poet, fated by his *métier* to early extinction. Orton would have delighted in all these Ortonesque details. He admired Firbank for his extraordinarily mannered language, and Feydeau for his exquisite construction, but most of all Oscar Wilde for his exemplary life of the poet. He believed that Wilde's style 'is much more earthy and colloquial than most people notice. . . . It's not glitter. . . . It's real – a slice of life'.

Perhaps with the example of Ben Jonson, the 'bricklayer of Westminster,' in mind, Orton aspired to be 'as tough as a bricklayer': 'There is this complete myth about writers being sensitive plants. They're not. It's a silly nineteenth century idea, but I'm sure Aristophanes was not sensitive' (Lahr, p. 126). How Orton could have known this is beyond our ken, but he wanted writers to be committed to real life: to pleasure, to the body – he himself was a body-builder who liked to anoint his body with oil – to laughter and to sex. He was proud that his 'authentic voice' was 'vulgar and offensive in the extreme to middle-class susceptibilities' (Lahr, p. 206). Finally, the Ortonesque is a vigorous assertion of hedonistic self-indulgence, polymorphous perversity and freedom from all cant.

John Russell Taylor concludes his disparaging and patronising chapter on Orton in *The Second Wave* with a grudging acknowledgement of his importance:

> But even on the humble level of providing commercial entertainment in the modern manner, what he did was unique, in its own way epoch-making, and surely entitles him to at least a footnote in even the severest histories of drama in our time. (p. 140)

Since this was published in 1971, Orton no longer seems to be merely a footnote in the history of modern drama but merits at least a significant chapter. His growing popularity must come as a surprise to many critics and reviewers, who thought of him as a slickly clever, commercial dramatist. In his introduction to *Entertaining Mr. Sloane* in Volume 8 of the Penguin Plays series, Taylor had already dismissed Orton with withering condescension as someone who knows 'what will and what will not go in the commercial theatre today', and whose *Sloane* is '*Arsenic and Old Lace*, 1964 model' (p. 12). How misguided that comparison now seems. Taylor damns Orton as a commercial dramatist who has set out 'to provide an evening's light comic entertainment', but, of course, 'living theatre needs the good commercial dramatist just as much as the original artist' (p. 13).

Understandably, these remarks infuriated Orton because he felt that he was being perversely misunderstood in favour of more bloodless and 'literary' playwrights. In fact, Taylor speaks of Orton as a 'good commercial substitute' for Arden or Livings. On the other hand,

Terence Rattigan's high praise for *Entertaining Mr. Sloane* embarrassed Orton because he had no way of reciprocating: 'It's like Rattigan's eulogies: I can't return them with any degree of conviction' (Lahr, p. 170). Orton thought of Rattigan with horror as the essence of a commercially successful playwright. Rattigan admired in Orton the naturalness and ease of his writing, a genuine brilliance in dialogue that seemed to come without any effort. Perhaps the most telling judgement of Orton's work is that of a fellow dramatist, Frank Marcus, who wrote *The Killing of Sister George*: 'I think it [*What the Butler Saw*] will survive and tell people more about what it felt to be alive in the Sixties than almost anything else of that period'.²

But if one considers Orton's brief career as a whole, there is an enormous development between *Ruffian on the Stair* and *What the Butler Saw*. Orton's naturalness did not come naturally, or, to put it another way, it took Orton a great deal of time and effort to realise that his writing need not be portentous, literary, allusive, or in any way connected with High Culture. The head games of *Head to Toe* disappear in Orton's later work. The point seems to be that, as in marathon running, if you run against the pain, the pain will disappear. Orton's later work is more fictional and less autobiographical. There is no attempt to insinuate either a personal cry of injustice or an indictment of society, as there certainly is in *The Good and Faithful Servant*. Rather, the experiential aspect is suppressed and the farce neutralises the pain. *Up Against It* ends as '*The sun streams into the room*' (p. 70); in *The Erpingham Camp* '*the body of* ERPINGHAM *is left alone in the moonlight with the red balloons and dying flames in a blaze from the distant stained glass*' (p. 320); and in *What the Butler Saw* all the characters '*climb the rope ladder into the blazing light*' (p. 448). Orton's apocalyptic fun is also 'mysteriously meant', and

Conclusion: The Ortonesque

we share in the characters' joyous epiphany. Farce relieves us of intellectual responsibility. Everything suddenly seems right, and we can enjoy ourselves without compromising our own deeply felt, black comedy instinct for disaster.

References

1. Introduction: The Life and Theatrical Career of Joe Orton

1. John Lahr, *Prick Up Your Ears: The Biography of Joe Orton* (New York: Knopf, 1978), p. 49. All subsequent material quoted from Lahr will be indicated in the text.
2. Joe Orton, *The Complete Plays*, introduced by John Lahr (New York: Grove Press, 1977), p. 67. All subsequent references to Orton's works will be indicated in the text, except for *Head to Toe*, *Up Against It* and *Until She Screams*, which are not included in this volume.
3. The Firbank influence is discussed in the doctoral dissertation of Gary Seigel, 'The Comedy of Joe Orton' (Rutgers University, 1981), which also takes up Pinter, Wilde and Feydeau.
4. 'Joe Orton Interviewed by Giles Gordon', *Transatlantic Review*, No. 24 (Spring 1967), p. 99.
5. Simon Trussler, 'The Biter Bit: Joe Orton Introduces *Entertaining Mr. Sloane*', *Plays and Players* (August 1964), p. 16.
6. See John Lahr's introduction to Orton's *Up Against It: A Screenplay for the Beatles* (London: Eyre Methuen, 1979), p. xi. All subsequent references will be indicated in the text.
7. Joe Orton, *Head to Toe: A Posthumous Novel* (London: Anthony Blond, 1971), p. 62. All subsequent references will be indicated in the text.

References

2. Sardonic Intellectualising in 'Head to Toe'

1. Orton, *Up Against It*, p. xii.

3. Stylistic Experiments: 'The Ruffian on the Stair', 'Funeral Games', 'Until She Screams'

1. The dates for Pinter, here and elsewhere, come from Bernard F. Dukore, *Harold Pinter* (London: Macmillan, 1982), in Macmillan Modern Dramatists series.
2. See John Russell Taylor, *The Second Wave: British Drama of the Sixties* (London: Eyre Methuen, 1978), pp. 126–7. Taylor comments shrewdly on the 'quite un-Pinterish direction' in which the play moves.
3. '*Until She Screams*: A Play by Joe Orton', *Evergreen Review*, No. 78 (May 1970), 51. All subsequent references will be indicated in the text.

4. Authority and Entertainment in 'The Good and Faithful Servant' and 'The Erpingham Camp'

1. See also Trevor Griffiths' play, *Comedians* (1975).

5. Occulted Discourse and Threatening Nonsense in 'Entertaining Mr. Sloane'

1. See Manfred Draudt, 'Comic, Tragic, or Absurd: On Some Parallels Between the Farces of Joe Orton and Seventeenth-Century Tragedy', *English Studies*, 59 (June 1978), 202–17. Leslie Smith in 'Democratic Lunacy: The Comedies of Joe Orton' (*Adam International Review*, No. 394–6 [1976], 73–92) makes a useful comparison between Orton and Jonson (p. 80). See also pp. 81 and 86.

6. 'Loot' as Quotidian Farce: The intersection of Black Comedy and Daily Life

1. See Eric Bentley, 'The Psychology of Farce', in his edition of *Let's*

References

Get a Divorce! and Other Plays (New York: Hill and Wang, 1958), pp. vii–xx, and his *The Life of the Drama* (New York: Atheneum, 1964). See also Barbara Freedman, 'Errors in Comedy: A Psychoanalytic Theory of Farce', in *Shakespearean Comedy*, ed. Maurice Charney (*New York Literary Forum*, Vols. 5–6, 1980), pp. 233–43.

   2. See Lahr, *Prick Up Your Ears*, pp. 195–7, and Albert Hunt, 'Arts in Society: What Joe Orton Saw', *New Society*, 17 April 1975, pp. 148–50.

   3. Hunt, 'Arts in Society: What Joe Orton Saw', p. 148. See also Leslie Smith: 'Orton brought farcical comedy, as no one else has done in quite the same way in our time, into creative relationship with the unconscious, and with some of the larger lunacies and nightmares of our time' ('Democratic Lunacy: The Comedies of Joe Orton', p. 92).

7. What Did The Butler See in 'What the Butler Saw'?

   1.   John Russell Taylor speaks slightingly of Orton's knowledge of 'how to put a play together in the manner of the moment without going too far and worrying Aunt Edna' (in the Penguin Plays collection that contains *Entertaining Mr. Sloane*; *New English Dramatists*, Vol. 8, p. 13). Orton knows how to titillate Aunt Edna without outraging her. *Entertaining Mr. Sloane* fitted only too well into the controversy about 'dirty plays' raging in London around 1964. See Pamela Hansford Johnson's novel, *Cork Street, Next to the Hatters: A Novel in Bad Taste* (London: Macmillan, 1965), in which a scurrilous and pornographic play that resembles *Sloane* is being staged. See also her reflections on the moral climate of the Moors murders, *On Iniquity* (London: Macmillan, 1967).

   The most outspoken of the moral attacks on Orton is by Martin Esslin in 'Joe Orton: The Comedy of (Ill) Manners' (*Contemporary English Drama*, ed. C. W. E. Bigsby, New York: Holmes & Meier, 1981, pp. 93–107). It is puzzling why Esslin should choose to write on a dramatist whom he so violently loathes socially, morally and personally, as in the following:

> Orton's rage is purely negative, it is unrelated to any positive creed, philosophy or programme of social reform . . . . he articulates, in a form of astonishing elegance and eloquence, the same rage and helpless resentment which manifests itself in the wrecked trains of football supporters, the mangled and vandalized telephone kiosks and the obscene graffitti on lavatory walls. Orton, one might say, gives the inarticulate outcries of football hooligans the polished form of Wildean aphorisms.   (p. 96)

Behind Esslin's own rage is the intensely snobbish conviction that Joe Orton is a 'yob', who expresses the rage of the socially and educationally under-privileged: having risen from the working classes of an ill-educated mass society that has lost all the religious and moral values of earlier centuries and has been debauched by the consumerism of a system manipulated by the mass media, Orton exemplifies the spiritual emptiness and – in spite of his obvious brilliance and intelligence – the thoughtlessness, the inability to reason and to analyse, of these deprived multitudes. (p. 107)

Esslin is the most articulate spokesman for the many respectable persons in Britain who were deeply outraged and affronted by Orton's plays, and, in a metadramatic sense, we seem to be listening to the voice of Mr McLeavy in *Loot*.

2. 'Joe Orton Interviewed by Giles Gordon', p. 96.

3. Throughout his career Orton was enamoured of the condensed, double-take paradoxes of Lewis Carroll. In his interview with Simon Trussler, for example, Orton opened with the Alice-in-Wonderland declaration: 'I hate all animals with tails'; Alice might have said just the opposite.

9. Conclusion: The Ortonesque

1. See Chapter 6, note 1.

2. Quoted in James Fox, 'The Life and Death of Joe Orton', *Theatre 71*, ed. Sheridan Morley (London: Hutchinson, 1971), pp. 67–8.

Bibliography

Writings by Orton

The Ruffian on the Stair, in *New Radio Drama* (London: British Broadcasting Corporation, 1966).

Entertaining Mr. Sloane (London: Hamish Hamilton, 1964; New York: Grove Press, 1964). New edition (London: Eyre Methuen, 1973).

Loot (London: Methuen, 1967; New York: Grove Press, 1967).

Crimes of Passion (revised version of *The Ruffian on the Stair* and *The Erpingham Camp*, London: Methuen, 1967).

Funeral Games and *The Good and Faithful Servant* (London: Methuen, 1970).

What the Butler Saw (London: Methuen, 1969; New York: Grove Press, 1970).

Until She Screams, in *Evergreen Review*, No. 78 (May 1970), 51–3.

Head to Toe (London: Anthony Blond, 1971; Panther paperback, 1971).

Joe Orton: The Complete Plays (London: Eyre Methuen, 1976; New York: Grove Press, 1977).

Up Against It: A Screenplay for the Beatles (London: Eyre Methuen, 1979).

Selected Criticism

Bigsby, C. W. E., *Joe Orton* (London: Methuen, 1982), in Contemporary Writers series.

Bibliography

Bryden, Ronald, 'On the Orton Offensive', *The Observer*, 2 October 1966.

Casmus, Mary, I., 'Farce and Verbal Style in the Plays of Joe Orton', *Journal of Popular Culture*, 13 (1980), 461–8.

Charney, Maurice, 'Occulted Discourse and Threatening Nonsense in Joe Orton's *Entertaining Mr. Sloane*', *New York Literary Forum*, 4 (1980) 171–8.

——, 'Orton's *Loot* as 'Quotidian Farce': The Intersection of Black Comedy and Daily Life', *Modern Drama*, 24 (1981), 514–24.

——, 'What Did the Butler See in Orton's *What the Butler Saw?*' *Modern Drama*, 25 (1982), 496–504.

Connell, Alexander, 'A Successful Prosecution', *The Library Association Record*, March 1963, pp. 102–5.

Draudt, Manfred, 'Comic, Tragic, or Absurd? On Some Parallels between the Farces of Joe Orton and Seventeenth-Century Tragedy', *English Studies*, 59 (1978), 202–17.

Esslin, Martin, 'Joe Orton: The Comedy of (Ill) Manners', in *Contemporary English Drama*, ed. C. W. E. Bigsby (New York: Holmes & Meier, 1981), Stratford-upon-Avon Studies 19, pp. 93–107.

Fox, James, 'The Life and Death of Joe Orton', in *Theatre 71*, ed. Sheridan Morley (London: Hutchinson, 1971), pp. 66–82.

Fraser, Keith, 'Joe Orton: His Brief Career', *Modern Drama*, 14 (1971), 413–19.

Gordon, Giles, 'Joe Orton Interviewed by Giles Gordon', *Transatlantic Review*, No. 24 (Spring 1967), 94–100.

Hunt, Albert, 'What Joe Orton Saw', *New Society*, 32 (1975), 148–50.

Johnson, Pamela Hansford, *Cork Street, Next to the Hatter's: A Novel in Bad Taste* (London: Macmillan, 1965).

——, *On Iniquity* (London: Macmillan, 1967).

Lahr, John, *Prick Up Your Ears: The Biography of Joe Orton* (New York: Knopf, 1978).

——, introduction to Orton's *The Complete Plays* (New York: Grove Press, 1977).

——, introduction to Orton's *Up Against It* (London: Eyre Methuen, 1979).

Loney, Glenn, 'What Joe Orton Saw: Death and the Maiden', *After Dark*, September 1970, 42–4.

Marowitz, Charles, 'Entertaining Mr. Orton', *The Guardian*, 19 September 1966.

Seigel, Gary, 'The Comedy of Joe Orton' (Doctoral dissertation, Rutgers University, 1981).

Shepherd, Simon, 'Edna's Last Stand, *Or* Joe Orton's Dialectic of Entertainment', *Renaissance and Modern Studies*, 22 (1978), 87–110. Special number on Popular Theatre.

Bibliography

Smith, Leslie, 'Democratic Lunacy: The Comedies of Joe Orton', *Adam International Review*, Nos 394–6 (1976), 73–92.

Spurling, Hilary, 'Early Death', *Spectator*, 18 August 1967, p. 193.

——, 'Young Master', *Spectator*, 14 March 1969, p. 344.

Taylor, John Russell, introduction to *New English Dramatists*, Vol. 8 (Harmondsworth: Penguin, n.d.), in Penguin Plays series. Contains *Entertaining Mr. Sloane*.

——, *The Second Wave: British Drama of the Sixties* (London: Eyre Methuen, 1978).

Thomsen, Christian W., 'Joe Orton und das englische Theater der sechziger Jahre', *Maske und Kothurn*, No. 19 (1973), 321–41.

Trussler, Simon, 'The Biter Bit', *Plays and Players* (August 1964), 16.

——, 'Farce', *Plays and Players* (June 1966), 56–8, 72.

——, article on Orton in James Vinson (ed.), *Contemporary Dramatists* (London, 1977), Appendix, pp. 984–6.

West, Nathanael, *The Dream Life of Balso Snell* (1931), in *The Complete Works* (New York: Farrar, Straus, and Giroux, 1966).

Worth, Katharine, *Revolutions in Modern English Drama* (London: G. Bell, 1973), pp. 48–56.

Index

Anderson, Lindsay, 19, 21, 23
Arden, John, 131
Aristophanes, 99–100, 107, 130
Arnold, Matthew, 3
autobiography, 3, 7, 11–12, 19, 41–3, 72, 83, 107, 118, 119, 130–1, 133

Bakhtin, Mikhail, 85
banality and clichés, 7, 15, 16, 19, 20, 21, 27, 66, 70–4, 76–9, 85–7, 94–5, 112, 114–16, 119, 121–2, 127–9
Bates, Michael, 18
Beatles, The, 1, 11, 15, 26, 27, 28, 97, 11–12, 117, 120
Beckett, Samuel, 41, 107
Bentley, Eric, 125, 135–6
Bigsby, C. W. E., 29, 30, 98–9
Boy Hairdresser, The, 6, 12–13
Brecht, Bertolt, 19, 61, 107, 112

Brooks, Mel and Carl Reiner, 10
Browne, Thomas, 40
Bryden, Ronald, 108
Burgess, Antony, *A Clockwork Orange*, 15
burlesque, 14, 40

camp and Kitsch, 10, 20, 41, 63, 113–15, 120–1
Carroll, Lewis, 12, 29, 34, 108–9, 137
Challenor, Detective Sergeant Harold, 94
Chatterton, Thomas, 130
Churchill, Sir Winston, 24, 63, 106
Cicero, 109
class consciousness, 5, 9, 59–60, 65, 125–7, 136–7
classical allusions, 12, 19–20, 30
collage, 71, 75–6, 79

Index

Collins Guide to Roses, 8
comedy of manners, 55, 79, 82, 123–4
Congreve, William, 18, 55, 108, 123
costume, 25, 30, 65, 100–1, 113, 114–15, 120–1
Cranham, Kenneth, 81
Crimes of Passion, 20

Defoe, Daniel, 60
detectives and murder mysteries, 8, 18–19, 22–3, 50, 88–94
Dickens, Charles, 59
Doyle, Arthur Conan, 89
Draudt, Manfred, 135
Dromgoole, Patrick, 15
Dukore, Bernard F., 135

Eliot, T. S., 98
Entertaining Mr. Sloane, 2, 3–4, 6, 11, 14–17, 20, 27, 30, 38, 55, 57, 62, 70–9, 82, 83, 91, 99, 105–6, 107, 109, 119, 126–8, 131, 134, 136
epigrams, 13, 22, 23, 47, 50, 72, 74, 78, 87, 116–18, 125–7
Epstein, Brian, 26, 111
Erpingham Camp, *The*, 2, 19–21, 24–5, 50, 52, 57–9, 63–9, 89, 92, 99, 118, 132
Esslin, Martin, 136–7
Etherege, George, 123
Euripides, *The Bacchae*, 19–20, 65, 99

farce, 14, 16, 17, 22, 23–5, 29, 34, 44, 46, 47, 49, 50,
52–5, 56, 57, 59, 71, 79, 81–2, 83–4, 85, 90–1, 95, 98–102, 104, 107–10, 112, 118–19, 121, 123–5, 129–30, 133, 136
father figures, 2, 119–20
Feydeau, Georges, 24, 82, 100, 108, 113, 125, 130, 134
films, 15, 19, 20, 21, 27, 64, 86, 90, 111–12, 115, 118–19, 120
Firbank, Ronald, 6, 12, 125, 130, 134
Fox, James, 137
Frazer, Sir James, *The Golden Bough*, 19
Freedman, Barbara, 125, 136
Freud, Sigmund, 77, 104
Funeral Games, 17, 21–3, 45, 49–55, 68

gags and jokes, 50, 51–2, 59, 67, 71, 84–5, 87–8, 119, 130
Gatsby, Jay, 3
Genet, Jean, 125
Gilbert and Sullivan, 87
Good and Faithful Servant, *The*, 2, 3, 4, 12, 16–17, 21, 52, 57–63, 66, 128–30, 132
Gordon, Giles, 8, 134, 137
Griffiths, Trevor, *Comedians*, 135

Halliwell, Kenneth, xi, 6–10, 13, 19, 27, 30, 31, 42, 75, 94, 118
Handke, Peter, 36
Head to Toe, 10–12, 27, 29–44, 112, 119, 121, 132, 134

Index

Heller, Joseph, *Catch 22*, 104
Holmes, Sherlock, 8, 88, 89
homosexuality, 2–3, 11, 15,
    25–6, 27–8, 38–40, 59, 71,
    72, 81, 84–5, 100, 102,
    113–15, 118, 124, 126
Hunt, Albert, 95–6, 136
Huxley, Aldous, *Brave New
    World*, 58

Ionesco, Eugène, 107, 109
Islington Borough Libraries,
    x, 7–9, 94, 118, 124

Jacobean tragedy, 48, 76,
    97–8
Jarry, Alfred, 89
Johnson, Pamela Hansford,
    136
Jonson, Ben, 130, 135

Kubrick, Stanley, 15

Lahr, John, 1, 3–5, 9, 16,
    18–20, 26, 71–6, 80, 83,
    84, 90, 94, 97, 99, 105,
    106, 108, 115, 123–7,
    129–32, 134, 136–7
Lamb, Charles, 18
language as weapon, 34–7
Lewenstein, Oscar, 111
library defacements, 7–9, 43,
    75, 94, 118, 124
Livings, Henry, 131
Lodge, David, 103
Loot, 3, 8–9, 12, 13, 17–19,
    22, 23, 26, 27, 30, 45, 50,
    52, 55, 57, 58, 80–96, 99,
    107, 108, 109, 119, 127,
    129, 130, 137

Maeterlinck, Maurice, 4
Marcus, Frank, 133
Marlowe, Christopher, 76, 98
Marowitz, Charles, 18
melodrama, 14, 23–4, 57,
    103, 119
middle-class values, 3, 8, 16,
    26, 35, 63, 66, 72–3, 79,
    82–3, 85–7, 88, 91–4, 97,
    114–15, 124–7, 131
Molière, 103
Monty Python's Flying Circus,
    33
mother/whore role, 14–15,
    72, 73, 76, 77, 82
music, 20, 66–7, 68, 75,
    129
music hall and vaudeville, 14,
    48, 62, 67, 113, 120

Nietzsche, Friedrich, 31, 99

Oh Calcutta!, 13, 55
onomastics, 32–3
Orton, Elsie, 2, 4, 72, 77,
    80–2, 95, 107
Orton William, 2, 10, 16, 59,
    72, 107
Orwell, George, *1984*, 58
Osborne, John, *The
    Entertainer*, 58

Pinter, Harold, 14–15, 20,
    45–9, 69, 71–2, 73, 83, 90,
    107, 112, 119, 121, 134,
    135
Plautus, 82, 99–100, 107, 125
politics, 21, 33, 59, 63, 65–6,
    67–9, 94, 119–20
polymorphous perversity, 11,
    24, 28, 37–8, 100–2, 106,
    107, 113–14, 121, 131

Index

pornography and obscenity, 8, 13, 45, 55–6, 84, 105–6, 118, 124, 136–7
Prick Up Your Ears, 123, 124
psychobabble, 85, 103–5

radio comedy, 67, 87–8
Rattigan, Terence, 132
real life and realism, 3, 18, 20, 59, 75–6, 77, 80–1, 83–4, 95–6, 108–10, 118, 130
religion, 21–3, 48, 49, 50, 52–5, 58, 62, 63, 64–6, 67–8, 83, 89, 104–5, 118
Restoration comedy, 55, 82, 102, 123
Rimbaud, Arthur, 130
Roth, Philip, *Portnoy's Complaint*, 77
Rothery, Madame, 5
Royal Academy of Dramatic Art, 5, 6, 8
Ruffian on the Stair, The, 6–7, 12–14, 20, 45–9, 83, 132

Schneider, Alan, 15–16, 128
Seigel, Gary, x, 134
sexuality, 11, 16, 24–6, 30, 33, 35, 37–40, 48–9, 51, 53, 55–6, 64, 67, 68, 73, 74, 75, 77–9, 81, 82, 84, 88, 98–106, 112–14, 117–18, 126, 127–8, 130
Shakespeare, William, 5, 8, 18, 31, 35, 39, 40, 48, 64, 75–6, 98, 103, 119, 129
Shaw, George Bernard, 27, 96
Shenson, Walter, 26, 111

Shepherd, Simon, 15, 58, 94–6
Sheridan, Richard Brinsley, *The Critic*, 123
Silver Bucket, The, 6, 27
Smith, Leslie, 135, 136
Sophocles, *Oedipus at Colonus*, 20
Southern, Terry and Mason Hoffenberg, *Candy*, 24
Stoppard, Tom, 32, 88, 105, 107, 109
Swift, Jonathan, 79
Synge, John Millington, 83, 96

Taylor, John Russell, 23, 95, 131, 135, 136
television, 16, 71, 77, 86, 128
Tourneur, Cyril, 76, 97–8
transvestism, 11, 25, 38, 100–2, 114–15
Trussler, Simon, 134, 137
Tynan, Kenneth, 13

Until She Screams, 13, 45, 55–6, 134, 135
Untitled Play, 13
Up Against It, 11, 15, 19, 26–8, 111–22, 132, 134

Violence, 15, 16, 29, 52–3, 58, 69, 72, 74, 90–2, 106, 124–5
Visit, The, 13–14
voyeurism, 39

Ward, Simon, 81
Welthorpe, Mrs Edna, 84, 105, 114, 124, 136

West, Nathanael, *Dream Life of Balso Snell*, 30

What the Butler Saw, 2, 11, 19, 23–6, 27, 28, 30, 34, 35, 45, 49, 50, 52, 53, 57, 63, 65, 74, 89, 97–110, 111, 112, 113, 120, 123, 126, 132

Wilde, Oscar, 55, 74, 79, 102, 108, 109, 116, 130, 134, 136; *The Importance of Being Earnest*, 23–4, 55, 85, 98, 108

Williams, Tennessee, 3, 107

women, 2–3, 38–41, 55, 77, 78, 102–3, 112, 113–15, 117–18

Wood, Peter, 18

wordplay, 51, 82, 103

working class, 2, 3, 9, 59, 66, 125–7, 136–7

Wycherley, William, 79, 123